PRINCIPLES OF THE
Stitch

PRINCIPLES OF THE Stitch

LILO MARKRICH

Henry Regnery Company • Chicago

Library of Congress Cataloging in Publication Data

Markrich, Lilo.
   The principles of the stitch.

   Bibliography: p.
   Includes index.
   1. Embroidery.   I. Title.
TT770.M37   1976   746.4′4   76-6271
ISBN 0-8092-8447-2
ISBN 0-8092-7964-9 pbk.

Published by Henry Regnery Company
         180 North Michigan Avenue
         Chicago, Illinois 60601
Manufactured in the United States of America
Library of Congress Catalog Card Number: 76-6271
International Standard Book Number: 0-8092-8447-2 (cloth)
                           0-8092-7964-9 (paper)

Published simultaneously in Canada by
Beaverbooks
953 Dillingham Road
Pickering, Ontario L1W 1Z7
Canada

Contents

For William L. Markrich (1914-1967) and our children.

Whatsoever thy hand findeth to do, do it with all thy might, for there is no work, nor device, nor knowledge, nor wisdom in the grave, whither thou goest.

Eccles. 9:10

ACKNOWLEDGMENTS

I am most grateful to my friends at the Textile Museum: Louise W. Mackie, Acting Director; Irene Emery, Curator Emeritus, Technical Studies; Ann P. Rowe, Assistant Curator, Western Hemisphere Textiles; Patricia Fiske, Assistant Curator; Clarissa K. Palmai, Conservator; Helen Kovacs, Associate Conservator; Anni Jackson; Ellen M. Beans; Nancy J. Wolf, Administrative Assistant; Pinar Arcan; and Sollie E. Barnes, Maintenance Superintendent, for suggestions, challenging comments, and their time to assure accuracy of statement and the correct presentation and mounting of the textiles photographed.

I am indebted to Anthony N. Landreau, former Executive Director of the Textile Museum and an authority on Caucasian village rugs, for his comments on rural industries in the Balkans; Dr. David Rogers of the Bodleian Library, Oxford, England; and Dorothy Mason, Reference Librarian Emeritus of the Folger Shakespeare Library for their advice relating to embroidered bookbindings and the manuscript of Thomas Trevelyon; Dr. Claus Ahrends of the Helms Museum, Harburg, Germany, for his suggestions relating to archaeological research in the Baltic; and to Klaus Tidow of the Textilmuseum in Neumunster for the generous use of his own research material; Dr. Esin Atil, Assistant Curator of Near Eastern Art, Freer Gallery, Washington, D.C., for her comments relating to Turkish textiles; and B. Norwick of New York for the use of his monograph on the origin of knitting.

My thanks to my uncle Mr. H. E. Kiewe of Oxford who generously provided me with unlimited access to his personal notes on the migration of folk patterns, his library, and his collection of embroidered materials, all three the culmination of a lifetime fascination with the style development of textiles; E. G. B. Milne; J. B. McKay of Oxford; my son Michael, my daughter Sandra, and my son-in-law Dr. H. B. Krebs for inevitably finding one more essential book; and L. R. Elliott and many of my students for providing one more example of needlework for my collection. Thanks to Christian M. Freer and Andre M. P. Shaw for translating Italian and Russian reference material.

The development and final form of the manuscript would have been impossible without Judith Conaway's enthusiastic support for the concept of the book; Nicole Taghert and Shirley Holmes; Louise Craven Hourrigan, who spent many hours on the illustrations; and the photography of Raymond Schwartz in Washington, D. C. and E. Palm of Oxford. I am grateful to Nancy Magee, Helen Whitmore, and James Parrill, who completed complex projects in record time so that I might make use of them while my daughter Julia Krebs-Markrich and my friends B. B. Kidder, Dr. Elizabeth Johnston, and Patricia G. Dubin contributed many hours of critical advice, typing, and editorial suggestions. To provide me with extra time, Jan Eiler and Louise Steele quietly substituted their efforts for mine at the Textile Museum Shop and young Jonathan was equally supportive at home.

To all of you—thank you.

FOREWORD

In establishing the Textile Museum in 1925, George Hewitt Myers made his huge collection of handwoven fabrics permanently available to everyone interested in textiles and rugs. Curators, collectors, and interested persons have been attracted to the museum in order to study and research its outstanding collections of ancient fabrics, which have been preserved through methods developed by conservators. The influence of the museum's training programs for young textile specialists has been felt in many textile collections in this country.

Catalogues of part of the museum's collections and exhibitions have been published, and one of its publications, *The Primary Structures of Fabrics* by Irene Emery, brought out in 1966, has become a major reference work for everyone interested in the classification of structure and the use of clear and meaningful terminology.

Today's needlework enthusiast often has not been exposed to the craftsmanship and artistry of past weavers and embroiderers nor to the importance of archaeological and ethnographic textiles as documents of the social history of mankind.

Lilo Markrich, a charter member of the Textile Museum Associates and the organizer of the Textile Guild, which services our Textile Museum Shop, shares in this book her broad knowledge gained through her many years of teaching classical embroidery in Washington, D. C.

It is our hope that this book will form a bridge between today's needleworkers and the fabrics that were carefully designed and worked in the past and thereby provide a greater understanding of this decorative art form that is important to us all.

Louise W. Mackie
Acting Director

Introduction

Stitches are the basis of embroidery—the embellishment of a previously woven fabric by means of a pointed tool (the needle) and fibers of organic or synthetic material (the thread). The skill of pulling a thread in and out and through a background material at different angles and tensions, and with different twists, layers, and textures, constitutes the art of stitchery.

The stitch has been an integral part of our cultural history. Needlework was refined into its present form as generation after generation transmitted the essential hand movements by demonstration, each generation contributing its own experience to the art. Developing a sense for the potential relationship between the woven background material and its decorative thread elements was a necessary part of every apprenticeship. There are no records of the way the first stitches were made, there can only be assumptions as to how they have evolved. But contemporary stitches most certainly have their roots in the early techniques used to structure basic fabrics. In her book *Primary Structures of Fabrics*, Irene Emery lists close to 300 thread or element manipulations by ancient and primitive cultures, all capable of producing a cohesive fabric. Such wide-ranging technical expertise, fully documented by textiles found on archeological expeditions, can hardly be attributed to chance. Rather, these fabrics are the sophisticated product of generations of craftsmen whose very livelihood depended on mastery of the skills involved.

Needlework owes its continuity as an art form in large part to those willing to support the professional artist. Textile remnants in today's museums are evidence of detailed, sophisticated projects originally commissioned by a wealthy and powerful religious or secular elite. Surely, there is no clearer indication of the importance of the embroidered textile than its long usage by the Christian church. Of almost unsurpassed excellence, technically and artistically, the relics of century-old ecclesiastical vestments, pouches, almsbags, and other church decorations manifest basic human aspirations through the medium of embroidery. Needlework was also kept alive by the centuries-old practice of passing down from generation to generation all essential domestic needlework skills, young workers painstakingly emulating their elders. With communities isolated from each other by distance and lack of communication, embroidery styles unique to particular regions gradually developed. These indigenous styles gave a distinctive flair to garments and textiles required for special occasions and to other household articles as well.

The Industrial Revolution radically altered both the role that stitchery played in people's lives and the way in which it was preserved for future generations. Suddenly, much of the work that had taken vast amounts of time and labor to produce could be made speedily and effortlessly by machine. In England, the first industrial world power, workers who had eked out a livelihood by their meticulous stitching of debutant gowns and elaborate shawls, found other ways of making a living in factories, shops, and offices while the workshop owners themselves turned to the sale of the mass-produced needlework supplies.

Toward the second quarter of the nineteenth century, a younger generation reacted against the already apparent disadvantages of the new industrial era and reevaluated embroidery as a craft relevant to art. The resulting Arts and Crafts Movement was made up of the literate and the artistic, the prophets of their time. These individuals understood the revolutionary impact of power-driven machinery on everyday life. They feared the extinction of craftsmanship in all areas, as the skilled artisans were pushed aside, unable to compete with the swifter, cheaper methods of mass-producing machine-made objects. The old-fashioned textiles—embroidered, woven, knitted, and looped—were being made obsolete by the unbelievably sophisticated and inexpensive machine-made copies which the newly affluent preferred. The Arts and Crafts Movement rejected the theory that the capabilities of the machine rendered negligible the abilities of working men and women. By founding museums or contributing to them, by collecting handmade decorative pieces for themselves and commissioning them, those interested in the art and craft of needlework helped provide a livelihood for artists, artisans, and craftspeople. By sponsoring

exhibits, supporting schools, and underwriting specialized publications, these people tried to preserve not only traditional skills but also old workbooks, samplers, and fragments of earlier textiles found in the possession of neglected artisans. Embroidered ecclesiastical vestments, garments, peasant blouses, ceremonial clothing, and other objects that documented the culture and civilization of an earlier period were sought out and protected against discoloration and decay.

The twentieth-century embroiderer has not been heir to a tradition of learning by doing, which is at the base of any craft. The embroiderer must now rediscover for himself a past as well as a technique that were lost irretrievably when the chain of transmitted knowledge about such things was broken by the Industrial Revolution. The needleworker is compelled to begin at the beginning once more to learn about both the history and the craft of embroidery. For historical facts, one has the increasingly documented research of archaeologists and anthropologists. For the development of embroidery as a personal craft, books and specialized instructors can suggest, stimulate, and encourage. But the development of personal skill depends upon one's own initiative. There are no rules that cannot be broken; the only rules are those dictated by one's sensibility, as the embroiderer develops an expertise, a feeling for his materials.

When I taught my first crewel embroidery class as part of a fund-raising project in Key West, I discovered that none of my students had ever before handled a needle for purposes of ornamentation. I gave a fleeting thought to referring to the traditional rules followed in twentieth-century needlework textbooks, but when I took handwork classes they had bored me, nearly stifling my interest in embroidery. Instead I had become fascinated by the interplay of fiber threads; weaving made me first aware that the secret to success in any field is the ability to cope with unexpected disasters.

Confident that my crewel class had enrolled with a generous amount of goodwill, common sense, and the ability to think, I began to teach this course from my own point of view.

This book is planned along the lines of my classes, which I continued to give when we moved to Washington, D. C. It does not seem necessary to me that students sit around a table working only one stitch at a time within a specified area. Instead I assume that individuals capable of coping with the intricacies of twentieth-century life are quite capable of making a stitch that requires little more than moving one's hands up and down in one way or another. The key to understanding the difference between one stitch and another—and the awareness that separates the beginner from the more advanced embroiderer—is the realization that the slightest variation of extended hand movement will produce subtle changes in the appearance of any one stitch.

The Illustrated Stitch

In 1967, when Irene Emery, now curator emeritus at the Textile Museum, published her long-awaited work, *The Primary Structures of Fabrics*, archaeologists, curators, collectors, artisans, and instructors were provided for the first time with a precise terminology with which to define textile structures. With this new vocabulary, the textile specialist is not only able to describe the form of a piece, the shape of a pattern, the color of a design, and the materials used, but can also detail the precise system by which the various fibers have been arranged. (I have used Irene Emery's terminology whenever possible as it ensures precise descriptions of stitches and stitching processes.) However, embroiderers have not always been so lucky. Books in the past have been incomplete, inadvertently misleading entire generations of needleworkers because they assumed a knowledge on the part of the reader that he no longer had. Since professional craftspeople had taught and had been taught by demonstration and repetition, the earliest embroidery books were probably pattern books, undoubtedly hand-drawn and only later, with the invention of movable type, printed for the commercial trade. How-to books published before the middle of the nineteenth century emphasized pattern rather than hand movement. Only occasionally does one come across an early book that describes in detail

which finger movement should be used, and even then the description is brief. Speed being of the essence to the professional, swifter stitch techniques were always jealously guarded. And in those early days, an encyclopedic knowledge of the hand movements required for every stitch was not nearly as important as a feeling for the materials to be used and the "mystery" of the craft.

Books describing how to make a stitch are a phenomenon of the Industrial Revolution. Two factors contributed to their appearance, the mass production of books, which made them inexpensive to buy, and the rise of a newly prosperous middle class, not compelled to produce domestic textile requirements. This combination of factors led to the first significant changes in the attitude toward needlework. With the increased leisure market, the publication of detailed stitch illustrations and instructions became commercially profitable. The prosperous wives and daughters of the new bourgeoisie could afford bought books and other publications that catered to their needs.

The new middle class, seeking guidance in good taste, ever ready to substitute a French name for an everyday object, eagerly purchased those books that promised to increase the "cultural level" of the reader. An interest in the historical details of needlework took hold, and collecting stitch patterns became an elegant pastime. But as mentioned before, these earlier books miscalculated how much their audience knew. Some of them, written in the form of encyclopedias by sophisticated and knowledgeable women, did combine stitch techniques and patterns to a degree; but they remained inadequately written for a public completely ignorant of needlework skills.

Publishers illustrated these earlier books with the most tasteful engravings, giving artists the license to make each detail more attractive than that actually possessed by the object. No textile was ever as precise in line, no stitch outline as delicately curved, nor a design as well-proportioned in relation to the width of the embroidery, as those shown in the illustrations of nineteenth-century how-to books. But these handsomely bound and fashionable publications, in spite of the clarity and excellence of their engraving, only told a partial story. The rest of the market was covered by cheaper and less-elaborate publications, distributed by large needlework companies producing fabric threads. These companies rightly saw in them a way to increase sales—the illustrations often represented merchandise manufactured by the company itself. Unfortunately, the suggested stitches and designs included in these publications catered to the public's taste for the simple-to-make. The reason behind that was, rightly, that work quickly finished would assure further sales. The specialized skill of decorating with stitches, always before subject to individual interpretation by gifted embroiderers, was now reduced to conform to the manufacturer's notion of what would sell the most.

Reacting to the glut of manufactured platitudes and trying to preserve handskills, men and women of the nineteenth-century Arts and Crafts Movement countered with their own books of instruction. However, they unwittingly compounded the problem.

As modern innovators in an age greatly influenced by the machine, the new writers on needlework organized, analyzed, tabulated, and regulated embroidery stitches within a rigid framework. To their precise minds, this seemed the only reasonable way to protect the future of needlework in a scientific-minded age. Yet they failed to see that the texts they were writing (and which, thanks to their social prestige, were unhesitatingly accepted) encouraged an embroidery of rote rather than one of imagination. Instead of alphabetical listings, these books stressed line and form; stitches were classified as flat, looped, and knotted. Their exact counterparts, used elsewhere on other fabrics or in other styles, were unnecessarily given different names and listed separately. This practice served not only to divide the stitches but to separate one embroidery form from another. And needlework stitches that could be adapted to any background suddenly became locked into categories.

It was only natural that a later generation, in the course of rediscovering needlework after years of neglect, would turn to these technically oriented publications and accept unequivocally their judgments and assumptions. Stitches

had to look like the drawings and be in perfect proportion to the threads used. The back was to be as perfect as the front. Certain stitches had certain functions and were not to be used in another manner. Deviations from such norms, however artistic the end result, simply indicated an ignorance of "good" embroidery.

But embroidery is neither rigid nor mysterious. Stitches are accessories to a fabric. They are grouped in this book not by shape and texture, but by the hand movements that form the root stitches. From a mere handful of root stitches, all other stitches originate. Though some stitches require more than one hand movement to complete, they can be executed without confusion simply by referring back to the root stitch.

The concern of this book is not to list all possible stitch variations, although customary names are included. Nor is it a description of the endless variety of historical, national, or regional styles. Rather, the book deals with the development and the structure of the most frequently used stitches. Only when the stitch is considered a tool—to be adjusted by angle, tug, or pull, with the emphasis on its capacity to enrich the embroidered design—will the quality of artistic workmanship be equal to that of the past.

The text deals with stitches based on the most simple hand movements (the oldest stitches), and the manner in which they lend themselves to shading. In addition, stitches are illustrated throughout in three different ways, the manner of presentation dictated by the information to be conveyed. Detailed drawings show essential stitch processes; simple straight lines are used to illustrate stitch variation; and photographs show the three-dimensional feel given the flat stitch by the quality of a particular yarn.

The Embroiderer

Embroiderers fall into three categories: the beginner, who usually views embroidery with awe and apprehension; the intermediate, who exercises a more critical ability; and the seasoned needleworker, whose judgment is swift and confident. These various reactions reflect different levels of understanding of the process that goes on in interpreting the original drawn outline into a finished piece of embroidered work.

The beginner's immediate reaction to a piece of embroidery often depends on its shapes and colors. For this reason, popular kit designs are brightly colored renditions of favorite motifs—flowers, landscapes, and pleasing stylized patterns. That a stitching process will actually result in such a visual image usually overwhelms the beginner, and is likely to produce feelings of inadequacy. The kits are thus designed to render artistic judgment unnecessary. This might be helpful at first (the author has reservations). However, their rigid program of do's and don't's should by no means constitute the only learning experience for the beginner embroiderer.

The intermediate worker is more self-possessed. He or she is aware that stitches are simply repetitive, controlled hand movements, and no more difficult to learn than any other alphabet. This needleworker already realizes that the stumbling block to good needlework is not *how* to make a stitch, but *where*, and with what color and texture. The intermediate understands the two basics of good needlework—the image and the technique—and is ready to explore both more fully. His or her willingness to conform to someone else's instructions and standards is gradually replaced by curiosity and a greater personal involvement.

A common incident that takes place during the stitching of a kit design is that the thread runs out, making it necessary for the embroiderer to purchase additional threads to either complete or change the color scheme of a kit. Since kits seldom encourage variation, the embroiderer, perhaps impatient with the predictability of the packaged design, is compelled to go his own way. He will then discover the shop that offers much more than just the packaged kit—one that offers a variety of interchangeable embroidery materials as well as a selection of stitch publications. As if a new world has opened to him, the intermediate needleworker will find himself attracted by museum exhibits of embroidered textiles. With increasing sophistication, the embroiderer begins to criticize works of embroidery, differentiating between stitches and between patterns. His confidence gives him greater flexibility, and he is no longer afraid to rip out unsatisfactory stitches in his own work and begin anew. The secret to success is the ability to cope with unexpected disasters.

A needleworker is experienced the day his hand movements become second nature to him, pure reflex. When this happens, the embroiderer is free to consider more fully the integrated relationship of design, color, texture and stitch workmanship. Stitches are much like musical composition. Stitches, together with the color of the threads used, are the melodic notes played against an accompaniment—the background material. This is neither a sentimental nor a romantic notion. The embroiderer works like a conductor. Being a master of technique, he or she orchestrates a blend of tonal harmonies and color. Just as the musician uses emotion to heighten or dull a tone, the embroiderer allows his feelings to guide him in his interpretation of a traced pattern. The embroiderer, like the musician, selects the sweep of his design.

The Fabric and Other Materials

Few beginners realize that the structure of the primary fabric influences the appearance of the stitch. In order to take advantage of the relationship between the primary fabric and the stitch element, one must understand the structure of the background primary fabric. Weaving is the interlacing of weft elements (horizontal threads) through taut warp (vertical) elements, the latter serving as a rigid framework that can be spaced closely together or far apart. (*See* figure 1.) The weaver interlaces vertical warp element by alternately moving the hand (and the shuttle holding the weft element) up and down, over and under, horizontally across the warp. On the second or "return" journey, the same up-and-down motion picks up during the *down* motion the previously crossed warp and crosses during the *up* movement the previously bare warp element. The weaver can control these elements to produce either a rough or smooth, open-holed (mesh) material or a closely woven and beaten opaque one.

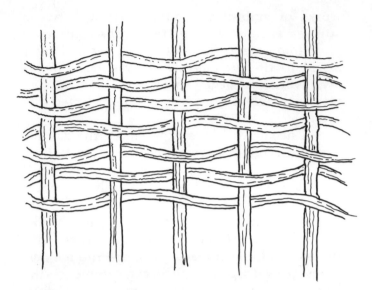

Figure 1. Plain weave. Five warp elements interlaced by seven weft elements. Elements are not equally spaced and therefore not balanced.

The regularity of an embroidery stitch, the evenness of its spacing, its width and length, depend upon the openness of the structure which serves as its framework and background.

When the worker uses a background material with an obvious warp and weft, such as needlepoint canvas or homespun, the openings between warp and weft elements become the needle's surfacing and re-entry points. They regulate stitch structure and contribute to the geometric shapes and systematic surface decoration of needlework styles such as needlepoint and counted thread work (cross stitch, etc.).

On the other hand, fabrics without an obvious weave do not intrude onto stitch structure and permit easy curving, and the use of unlimited varieties of embroidery elements and patterns. In this case, the fabric and its color serves as a backdrop to offset the needlework.

In order to discover for yourself the influence of fabric on embroidery, it is necessary to have on hand a variety of different primary fabrics—both coarse and fine, woven from cotton, linen, wool, and synthetics—as you read this book, so that the transition of a stitch from one style to another can be practiced. Use a sturdy Indian Head cotton or a homespun for free form work. Don't even bother with the flimsy fabrics; unbleached muslin for example, is too weak.

Using more than one type of embroidery element will emphasize differences in texture. Just by changing from a rough wool to a smooth silk or cotton you will become more aware of the difference between two embroidery styles.

A hoop will be needed for some work and a ballpoint laundry marker with guaranteed waterproof ink is also required. Do not be tempted by just any felt-tipped pen. Dressmaker carbon, a knitting needle, and graph tracing paper (in sizes to match whatever needlepoint canvas swatches you have) are other useful items to have on hand.

Suggestions

Pay attention to how stitches and patterns are drawn so that you don't get confused. Uneven numbers always mark all surfacing movement from backface to frontface of the primary fabric. The squares of graph paper, if blocked out to show a pattern or shape, will indicate *one complete stitch* up *and* down. For canvas stitches based on multiple hand motions, the holes represent the space where the needle comes up, and the grid lines are the warp and weft elements of the primary fabric which have to be crossed.

Stitches are not grouped by their texture but by the dominant hand movements required. Therefore, some stitches will be identical in appearance on the frontface of a primary fabric, but the stitch structure will be different at the backface; structural variations do alter the tension and thereby the appearance of a stitch.

The tug and pull that each individual gives to the needle as it pulls the embroidery element through the primary fabric is as personal as his handwriting and affects the appearance of any stitch. Uneven tension will produce uneven stitch structure; even rhythm of tug and pull will produce a uniform one.

Don't hesitate to write marginal notes to yourself concerning your reactions to particular stitches or exercises. The notebooks of past craftsmen with their notations in pencil and ink are treasured as an additional source of information. Indeed your own notes will serve to refresh your memory in future projects.

Don't feel that you must produce a sampler that is a work of art. Samplers as pictorial school drills were an 18th-century pheno-menon; before that they served simply as stitch pattern reminders. Don't worry about irregularity of stitching and don't think that the museum pieces worked by five-year-olds were always exhibition work. Rough experimental work was neither saved nor shown. Try to regain the touch and feel for a medium which has been lost over the past century and remember that you are *not* a machine but a human being. (*See* figures 2 and 3.)

Consider every error a step forward and not a lack of ability. Without errors, one doesn't learn. Begin to understand that a stitch is like a chameleon, changing its appearance to suit its environment. The driving force behind the experienced amateur striving for excellence and perfection can be a stumbling block to the beginner. All that really matters is that you begin to develop a feeling of personal satisfaction as your efforts produce visible results. Enjoy your needlework. It can be fun!

Figure 2. Darning sampler 1849. North Germany. Textilmuseum—Neumünster, West Germany.

Figure 3. Late 19th-Century Sampler. Belgium convent curriculum, done by a student, May Curd, 1895-98 (May Curd later became the Mother Superior of a convent in England). One of the textbooks used was Encyclopédie des Ouvrages de Dames par Thérèse de Dillmont.

a. Buttonholing.
b. Cross stitch. Alphabet, name, and date started and finished.
c. Sewing details.
d. Padded satin.
e. Appliqué on net with satin stitch.
f. Buttonhole on net.
g. Cut work Brodere Renaissance.
h. Satin stitch and laid stitch. Art Needlework.
i. Le Filet.
j. Church embroidery. French knots and stem stitch.
k. Le Filet II.
l. Tambour work.
m. Brodere Anglais.
n. Net (Tulle) embroidery. "Point Damasse." Note the small squares of white on white tent stitches on linen.
o. (1) Drawn threadwork, including satin stitch and pattern darning. (2) "Les Jours sur Toille" or openwork on a woven background.
p. Ribbons joined by crochet-lace insertion, embroidered details.
q. Darning. Le Raccommodage.
r. Net appliqué with tambour lines.

1 The Running Stitch

The stitch is deeply rooted in the framework of civilization. Men, women, and children throughout history have woven their own skirts and shirts, bandings and purses, and other functional objects. Whether these woven objects are everyday clothing or ceremonial costumes, many have been sewn and embroidered with stitches that reflect the traditional preferences of the people.

In the eighteenth and even in the nineteenth century, villages were at the mercy of the eccentricities of nature for their survival. Used to coping with the quirks of nature, the inhabitants of isolated villages absorbed the new gradually, but never abandoned the tried and true. They thereby preserved for the twentieth century, traditional cultural practices that, with the advance of industry and technology, might have otherwise been lost.

Today it is fascinating to watch needle-workers in unindustrialized areas practice their native skills. They weave and embroider with deft, smooth motions, taking for granted their mastery of traditional hand movements. Their creative energy is thus focused on the forms and shapes used as decorative motifs. In the past, these emblems were frequently devised to protect the object's owner from evil spirits. These emblems also identified villagers with a particular tribe, religion or nation. Today, they are preserved as historical artifacts for the region and period in which they were produced. There are many similarities in all ancient works of embroidery even though they issue from different geographical areas. Whether these similar skills and designs arose independently from each other or whether they originated from a single source will be answered in time by the work of archaeologists. Nevertheless we know that needlework eventually became valued as an object of trade. This made it possible once again for another group of craftsmen to earn their living by their skill as embroiderers, freeing them from having to work on the land. As the cultural gap between the rural community and the town widened the needs of the prosperous and the powerful increased. The towns and cities looked to the villages to supply them with additional labor. The village artisan and the skilled craftsman were eagerly sought out

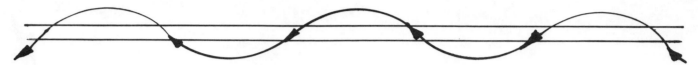

Figure 4. Upward and downward movement of an embroidery or sewing element as it interlaces with a previously woven primary fabric.

by royal and urban professional workshops. In his new and sophisticated environment, the villager learned to refine his techniques and to improve his product, diminishing the time required for its completion. If successful in town, the villager joined the urbanized middle class.

New fashions gradually filtered back into the village, thanks in part to the local landlords' practice of employing dependent village labor to produce their woven, sewn, and embroidered household items. The villagers then combined the new designs with the traditional styles of embroidery on the ceremonial linens and costumes they sewed for their families.

The Running Stitch in History

For centuries, both the professional and the amateur in town and village have used the least demanding but still effective ornamentation techniques to decorate their hand-woven, even-weave fabrics. This is the most basic of all stitches, known today as the running stitch.

The running stitch is a continuation of the basic up-and-down stitch which resembles the weft element as it crosses the warp. The embroiderer duplicates the weft as it runs across the warp and thus creates an ornamental accessory to the woven fabric. This movement ap-

pears on the primary fabric as a line of stitches interrupted by spacings. (*See* figure 4.)

Some fragments of woven stitched cloth discovered along the northern coastline of Europe (carefully analyzed by Claus Tidow of the Textilmuseum of New Münster, Germany) contribute to the historical documentation of the running stitch. These fragments, discovered in Feddersen Wierde, are thought to have been woven during the period of 50 B.C.-100 A.D. The survival of these fragile textiles is practically a miracle, since the area is known for its cold, damp, and salty bogs.

To judge these fragments—not by their looks, but by the spinning and ply of wild domesticated animal fibers, by the set of the weave, and by the joining of their seams—in relation to the physical energy and time required for bare survival, is to realize that the workmanship indicates a degree of civilization not generally recognized in that area for that time. It is evident from the carefully marked diagrams of the Textilmuseum-Neümunster (*see* figure 5) that, based on the hardened needle indentations and stitch fragments, the running stitch, together with other stitch techniques, was well known. Workers were already well aware that by alternately moving a needle from

Figure 5. Four examples of running stitch variations as found in the textiles of Feddersen Wierde.

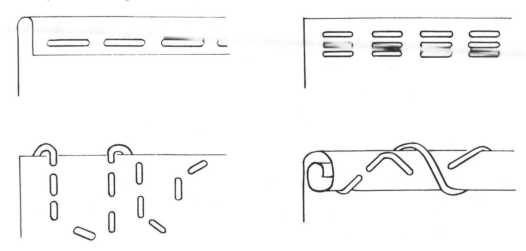

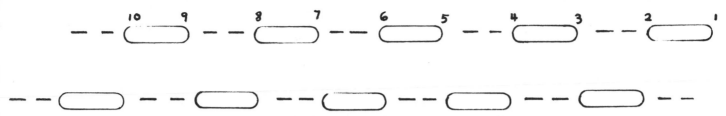

Figure 6. Raising at #1 and lowering arm and hand at #2 are the only hand motions required to simulate a weft interlacing on a primary fabric and to provide the embroiderer with the most simple needlework stitch, commonly known as the *running stitch*.

the backface of the primary fabric toward the frontface (up) and covering a certain number of warp elements before re-entering the frontface to return to the back (down) and then picking up the equivalent number of warp elements at the back before returning to the frontface, a regularity and evenness of stitch and space could be achieved. They are as precise and even as a weft crossing the warp, with the needle and hand imitating the weaver's shuttle as it crosses from side to side.

This technique, rather than serving as a decorative addition, was probably first used to reinforce a previously woven textile as it began to thin. Stitches identical in appearance to the weft would have unobtrusively helped preserve a woven object frayed by time. The romantic view, which assumes that the northern caveman invented the stitch to add a running line of color to his leather coverings, seems a little far-fetched, especially since markings on leather can be gotten by the simpler means of stamping or gouging.

The Domesticated Running Stitch

The name *running stitch* may have originated as a result of its use in joining two fabrics in a constant forward movement. Its main functions are to seam and sew with even spacing and stitch length, as well as to position two fabrics to be placed with their *right* sides facing one another. For greater speed in sewing, the two fabrics are correctly aligned and draped across the left forefinger. They are held in position by the thumb, while the right hand slides the needle up to the front and down to the back in a regular rhythm. (*See* figure 6.) When stitches and spacing are long and irregular, the same forward up and down technique is called *basting*.

The sewing stitch becomes decorative when the primary fabric is stretched taut and a second contrasting, smaller and shaped fabric is applied or appliquéd. The backface of the secondary fabric is laid on the frontface of the primary one. Then the even-spaced even-sized running stitch, its size adjusted to shape and need, is worked close to the edge of the secondary fabric. However, instead of gliding along as it follows the needle, the element is given a steady up and down tug as the needle moves through both fabrics. The effect of the stitch changes immediately. As a result of the tautness of the element on the surrounding primary fabric, a slight shadow at each entry and exit point frames the individual stitch. This is a matter of major importance when the running stitch becomes the essential joining and decorative quilting stitch. These darker shadow-breaks can contribute to or detract from any stitch's appearance unless taken into consideration. In quilting, for instance, the running stitch can become a positive decorative feature at the frontface of the outer fabric; the lines representing a motif can be intensified by the close spacing of shadow-breaks if very short stitches are used.

When the running stitch is worked along a piece of primary fabric in longer than necessary stitches, and the fabric is pushed back towards the first stitch, a fullness of material called *gathering* results. The running stitch in this instance has become a means of shaping in addition to its use in joining, mounting, and layering fabrics.

But it is in the realm of darning that the running stitch has for centuries been known to contribute richness and ornamentation. Darning is a process by which original, worn primary fabric is replaced with a patch. First, a

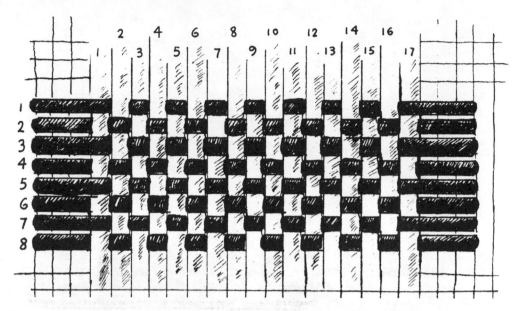

Figure 7. By varying stitch length and counting the number of primary fabric warp and weft elements to be crossed or picked up, the running stitch changes its name to pattern-darning stitch or surface darning. Pattern darning over and under one—plain.

framework of long parallel stitches is placed vertically as a substitute warp; then, the weft element is duplicated by moving a needle over and under the "warp" in an alternating horizontal row sequence (darning). (*See* figure 7.) This technique was later used in lace fillings and great ornamental pieces of embroidery, when it was given the additional name of *cloth stitch* or *point de reprise*. *Needleweaving* would be more appropriate.

Ornamental Darning

Ornamental darning has two pattern variations. The difference is both a visual matter and a matter of economics. Rural embroideries generally used the first variation. Within a single row, each stitch is methodically lengthened and shortened as the element crosses the frontface of the primary fabric. (*See* figure 8.) The length of the embroidery element covering the frontface of the primary fabric will produce a reciprocal uncovered space at the backface. Stitches picked up at the back will be equalled by spaces of identical size at the frontface. The needleworker can use this running stitch characteristic to frame the patterning on the frontface with the texture and color of the primary fabric. The pattern results from the carefully planned interplay of the embroidery element and the primary fabric. Note that front and

backside are only completely reversible if stitch and spacing are equal in width at all times. (*See* figures 9 and 10.)

There are several sound advantages to darning be it domestic or professional needleweaving. Actual pattern-weaving on a handloom is a highly skilled, time-consuming craft; decorated brocaded fabrics have always been expensive due to the detail required for the weave. However, before the machine age, the master of a professional workshop probably employed cheap female labor for this semi-skilled work. Decorative patterning would then be limited to essential areas and applied horizontally, vertically, or diagonally, depending on the fashion. The effect was similar to weaving and the cost was less. (*See* figure 11.)

In the villages of flax-growing areas of Europe, the carefully spun and woven linen stored in dowry chests ready for a daughter's wedding could acquire a touch of luxury with the addition of simple darning. The challenge of color and design gained a new pleasurable aspect. (*See* figure 12.)

Not all pattern darning is worked with the frontface of the primary fabric facing the worker. The Phulkari of the Punjab and other Far-Eastern pattern darning is worked with the backface of the primary fabric facing the worker. (*See* figure 13.) This has two advan-

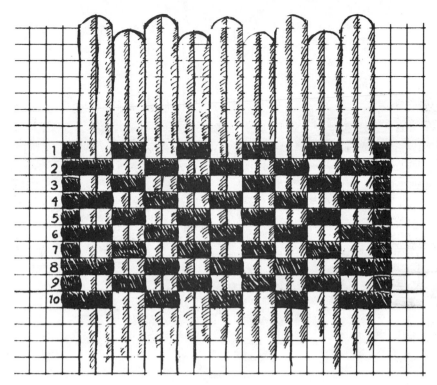

Figure 8. Pattern darning over and under two—stitch begins to float.

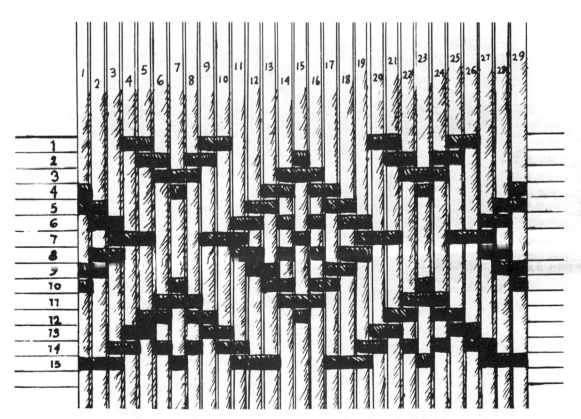

Figure 9. Pattern darning simulating weft floats as the length of the visible stitch is adjusted by the number of warp or weft elements it crosses.

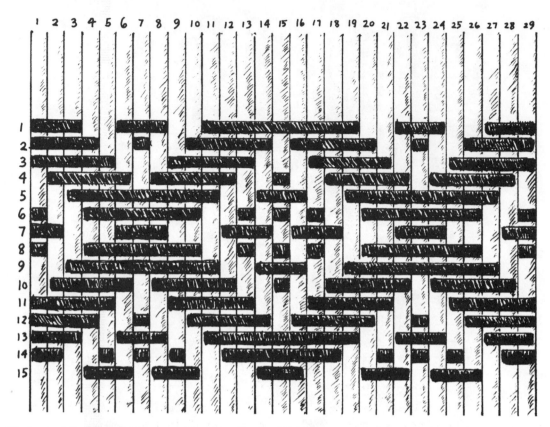

Figure 10. Reverse of figure 9. Pattern produced by the invisible stitches of the backface.

Figure 11. Pattern darning variations.

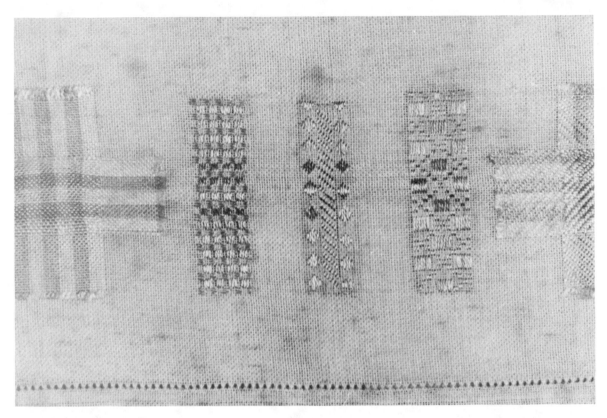

Figure 12. Darning. Le Raccommodage. A portion of May Curd Sampler. (*See* figure 3.)

Figure 13. Detail of Phul Kari pattern darning. (Left) backface detail. (Right) frontface. (Author's collection.)

Figure 14. Greek Island darning—"Naxos." TM 81.2 v64-1389.

tages. The first is that the customary silk floss is protected from constant handling and rubbing as the longer darning element float moves across the frontface. The second advantage is that greater visual accuracy is possible because the worker can use the dark, loosely-woven, weft element as the darning row's horizontal guideline. The expanding width of an individual soft-silk row would extend beyond its allotted range and cover the weft guideline of the next row, if long stitches were worked on the frontface. It is therefore easier to use the small weft covering backside floats of silk as a counting device. On the decorative side of the fabric, these backside floats of silk appear as small, primary fabric breaks interrupting a series of long floats. (*See* figure 14.)

In Balkan and Far Eastern areas where pattern darning involved finely-woven linen or cotton, and a more firmly-plied element, counting on the frontface of the primary fabric was simplified by working pattern rows in an alternating sequence. The missing stitch rows were completed later.

Kogin darning of Japan and the gold pattern darning characteristic of the Medieval ecclesiastical embroideries are other distinctive darning needlework fashions. All styles of pattern darning have one great advantage in common—the wonderful sheen and reflection produced by the play of light on the darning element as it rests with unobscured flatness on the surface of the primary fabric. The technique is easy to master. And darning elements too weak to withstand the push and pull of more demanding textile structures may be used.

2 Double Darning

In the collection of the Textile Museum in Washington, D. C., there is a beautiful rectangular panel filled with vibrant tulips, carnations of blue and red, sprigs of white and pink daisy-like flowers with soft green leaves and stems. The panel was made during the sixteenth and seventeenth centuries and is of Turkish origin. One stitch only, known as double darning, has been used throughout the piece. (*See* colorplate 1.)

By combining the texture of the primary fabric perfectly with the weight of the silk embroidery element, and by selecting a versatile stitch and using it well, the skilled Turkish needleworker has demonstrated that superior embroidery does not depend on the use of multiple stitches.

The double darning stitch is a running stitch modified to produce a solid reversible line of color in contrast to the previously mentioned pattern darning method.

Double darning is a literal definition of the technique used in the Turkish textile. A row of running stitches is worked from right to left, vertically from top to bottom, or towards the worker. At the end of the row, without turning the work (though, if convenient, there is no reason why one cannot), the embroidery element returns to the beginning of this first line of stitching. It then crosses the previously open spaces, picking up the previously worked thread lines. Thus a single line of color is produced, broken only by shadowed indentations.

With the use of light-reflecting elements such as silk or metallic thread and a good quality wool with sheen, the knowledgeable worker can manipulate this double-darning technique to such a degree that the stitch "breaks," or shadows multiply, producing variations on a solid color. In the Turkish panel mentioned above, each stitch crosses two weft elements, which is equal to three holes. The straight rows of small stitches run close to and parallel one another in the outward direction of each petal. Stitch lines in leaf and curving stalks sometimes run vertically, sometimes horizontally, and sometimes in a slant, whichever direction will give a maximum impact considering the varied play of light on the silk. Lines of double darning may be slightly staggered by raising or lower-

Figure 15. Fragment from Peru, possibly south coast. It may be Nasca style, ca. 200 B.C.-600 A.D., plain weave (cotton) embroidered with double running stitch (wool). TM 91.208. Courtesy of The Textile Museum

ing an adjoining row, and by filling areas not covered by the original line with additional small stitches. In this way, the light reflected will not be altered.

A factor of major importance occurs in the execution of the double-darning stitch whenever two stitches share the same hole of the primary fabric. The needle with the guest element dislodges the host element when entering the hole, and pushes it either to the right or left. In a continuous-line sequence, the work would appear irregular if the host element were randomly dislodged. To prevent this potential flaw in workmanship, the needle must routinely come up to the right of a previously worked stitch and go down to the left of the next host stitch. (See figure 18.) By conscientiously repeating this pattern, the double-darning stitch will acquire a slightly plied or twisted effect. When the worker is conscious of

the advantages and disadvantages of this technique, it can be used to flatten and broaden a shape's appearance.

Various Double-Darning Effects

To vary the effect of the double-darning stitch, vary its execution. A longer stitch using five or seven holes and crossing three or five weaving elements has a more definite appearance. If all subsequent alternating lines of double darning are begun midway to the previous row's bottom or top stitch, rows of double darning acquire a brick-pattern effect.

When a flat look is required, with definite horizontal or vertical shadow lines interrupting the motif, stitches must be adjusted so that all rows of double darning start and stop at the same level. Then horizontal lines of double darning will be broken by vertical shadow lines, and vertical rows by parallel horizontal shadow lines. This effect can be turned to good advantage by raising or lowering lines of double darning in a definite sequence. (*See* figure 15.) Returning to the oval form of a leaf shape, one can very easily obtain a veining effect, for instance, by working a line of double-darning first down the center of the leaf, to set the sequence. Place your second row of double darning one hole higher either to the left or to the right of this line. Continue parallel to this second row, each time moving one hole or one step higher. When the first half of the leaf is finished, return to the other side and repeat the same row sequence. The double-darn filling of the leaf shape will now be broken by a series of matching diagonal lines.

By staggering and grouping, endless variations can be obtained as long as the worker remembers that horizontal lines of stitching are broken by vertical shadows. Similarly, vertical rows are broken by horizontal shadow lines and diagonal lines are crossed by an opposite line of shadow markings. It is such details as these that one absorbed after a certain degree of stitching had been mastered during an apprenticeship. (*See* colorplate 2 and figure 16.)

Holbein Stitch

The reversibility of a technique such as double darning is particularly useful in embroidering a transparent or fragile primary fabric because it prevents the shadowy element on the backface showing through the fabric and blurring the desired effect. The use of the double-darning stitch to produce a duplicate pattern on each side of a primary fabric results in a geometric style of ornamentation popularly known as the Holbein stitch.

Explanations for the name vary. The most

Figure 16. Detail from colorplate 2. Tree trunk single-darning detail within a double-darning embroidery.

Figure 17. Detail of colorplate 3. Double darning. Note similarity in technique to English "blackwork" or "Holbein". Double running stitch relates to figure 20.

popular explanation is that the stitch was named after Holbein the Elder and Holbein's son, the famous painters of the fifteenth and sixteenth centuries. The Holbeins based their work on religious themes and were backed by wealthy patrons in Germany, Switzerland, and England. Both displayed a realism of style in the exquisite photographic detail of their work. They liked to paint black geometric patterning on their subjects' clothing: white veils, scarves, bodices, collars, and cuffs. The Holbeins might have placed their embroidered patterns in their portraits simply as decorative detail; but since it is believed that the Holbeins tried to increase their income by supplying embroiderers' workshops and private patrons with specialized needlework designs, it is therefore reasonable to assume that the Holbeins were the creators of this type of needlework.

Though these two artists have given their name to the Holbein stitch, it is important to notice that the motifs of the Turkish embroidery are outlined with single rows of double darning in the Holbein manner. Another fascinating textile from Peru (300 B.C.) in the Textile Museum certainly predates Holbein Elder and Son. The use of their name therefore defines not a stitch technique but a style. (See colorplate 3 and figure 17.) In 1873, in an effort to promote an exhibit of their paintings at the Kunsthistorisches Museum in Vienna the director of the Imperial Arts and Crafts School first drew the public's attention to the technique as the *Holbein* stitch, pointing out the similarity between the painted embroidery details and the then current nineteenth-century fashion of double-darning needlework.

The Holbein-stitch style was unusual because it used only two colors—the white primary fabric and the black silk embroidery element. In addition, the formerly horizontal (or vertical) lines of double darning (or double running) became angular, and the angle of the needle changed its direction as it made its forward and return trip so that each line became a combination of horizontal, vertical, or diagonal stitches. Single row outlines became boxed pyramids. Curves were no longer rounded but angular. The versatility of this well-defined stitch knew no limit as a geometric patterning device. (*See* colorplate 4.)

It has been said that Catherine of Aragon, the first wife of Henry VIII, introduced the fashion of black-on-white embroidery to England. But this is doubtful since the English had had many connections with the continent for centuries. This form of needlework must have been known before royal preference made it

fashionable. However, the black-on-white became so popular at the time of Henry VIII that other well-known stitches were used in such patterning and gold and silver elements added. English blackwork became a unique adaptation of the continental fashion.

Holbein work requires precision. Individual threads are counted when the eye can see the warp and weft elements. Otherwise a practiced eye allows the worker to cross and pick up identical amounts of the transparent primary fabric. The stitch instructions and worked samples clearly show the ease and elegance of the resulting work.

THE EVOLUTION OF THE PLAIN RUNNING STITCH

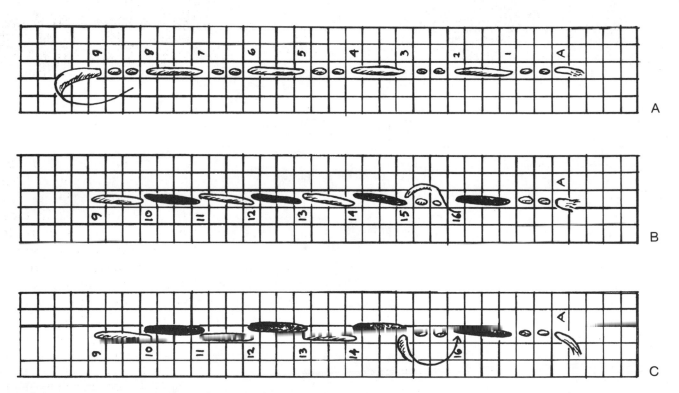

Figure 18. Double darning. Stitch lines can be worked in vertical and horizontal lines. (A) The needle first surfaces at #1, returns to the backface at #2. (To avoid knots on two-sided identical patterned embroideries the working element is first "run-in" as shown—the loose end will be covered and caught by the second set of stitches.) The difference between the two methods of double darning shown depends upon the way the needle will enter and resurface into the holes shared with the previous line of stitches. (B) In this method, known as twined double running, the working element at #10 surfaces to the right of the previous stitch and returns to the backface at #11 to the left of the next stitch. By continuing in this imperceptibly slanted manner, the two stitches appear to wrap around one another and the resulting solid line of color will be smooth and soft. This is the technique used in colorplates 1 and 3 from Turkey and Persia in the Textile Museum collection. Pessante is a popular name for the stitch. (C) Instead of a smooth line, a geometric roughness results when the second set of stitches enter or resurface consistently to the right (or left) of the first set of stitches.

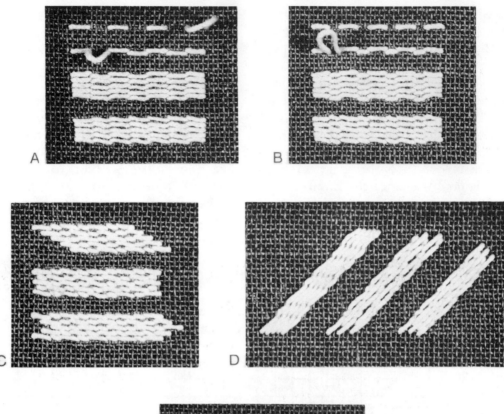

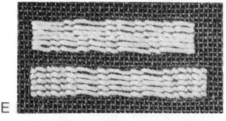

Figure 19. Examples of double darning using the methods described in figure 18.
    (A) 1st group: even spaced stitch.
           2nd group: even spaced stitch returning by using 18C.
           3rd group: even spaced stitch returning by using 18B.
    (B) 1st group: uneven spaced stitches.
           2nd group: uneven spaced stitches returning with 18C.
           3rd group: uneven spaced stitches returning with 18B.
    (C) Three horizontal variations (18B).
    (D) Three diagonal variations (18B).
    (E) Two horizontal pattern variations (18B).
    (F) Two pattern variations. (18B).

Figure 20. (A) Simple combination of straight vertical and horizontal stitch-lines. Such a finished line is called *battle-mented.* For diagonal lines (B) stagger stitch sequence as lines move down and up. In the photo (C) the first step is at the left, top-corner. Note that the second stitching line is an upward-moving row of vertical stitches. Horizontal lines on the frontface do not appear until the 3rd and 4th steps. To avoid pattern distortion, more complex patterns combining several variations sometimes require a double stitch at the end of a line to assure a correct return sequence.

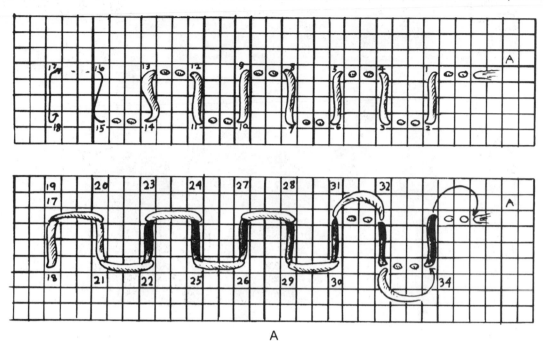

A

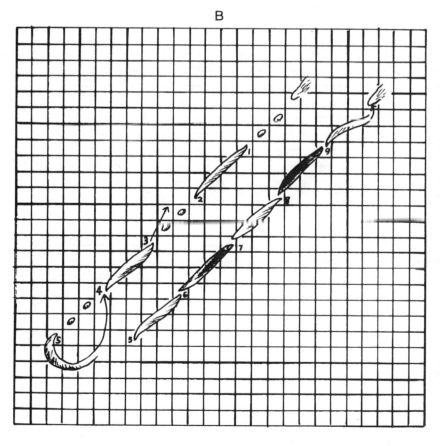

B

C

Figure 21. Double darning used as a filling stitch. Note how a horizontal shadow-break line divides rows of vertical stitching while staggered stitch-lines are crossed by diagonal shadow-break lines. The latter, properly spaced, can be used as veining within a leaf. Precise, even-spaced, double-darning lines provide angular two-faced outlines of identical appearance. This is often known as Holbein work. Its precision is assured when the primary fabric permits an easy counting of its weft and **warp** elements.

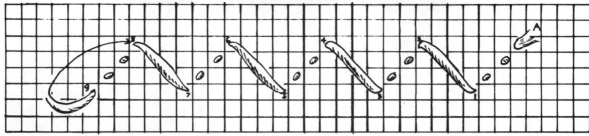

A

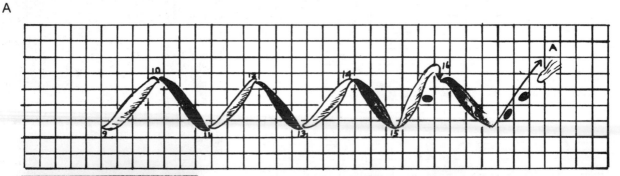

B

Figure 22 (A & B). Two opposing diagonal lines not only provide a series of interesting variations as seen in the photograph, but should be of special interest to needlepoint enthusiasts interested in a reversible canvas fabric (bags, belts, etc.). *See* figure 12.

Figure 23. Reversible canvas stitching. (A) Work a single line from right to left and shift to a reverse hand-motion and return below the first line in a staggered sequence. Repeat for all horizontal lines of stitching. Depending upon the amounts of solid color required there are two methods for filling the resulting vertical blank spaces. (B) Although awkward in movement this is the most flexible method for controlling smaller solid-color areas. The blank spaces are filled with the same stitch but this time the lines are worked vertically from top to bottom. Although it is possible to work upwards, in reverse motions, it is more time-consuming. (C) Turning the work sideways (first horizontal row becomes right-hand-side outer edge) all spaces can again be filled by horizontal lines of stitching. This method limits patterning to intersecting stripes (plaid). Drawbacks: This technique does not lend itself to large areas of solid-color canvas work as variations of tug and pull will result in an uneven stitch-row appearance. Multicolors and resulting stripes will diminish the visibility of irregular tension. Allowances must be made to dovetail adjoining color lines, as no two rows can finish at the same edge.

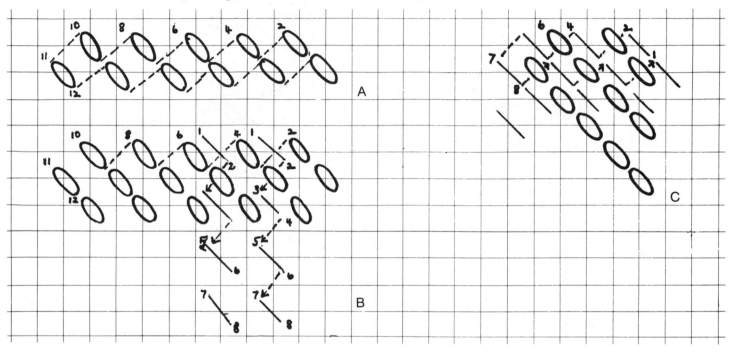

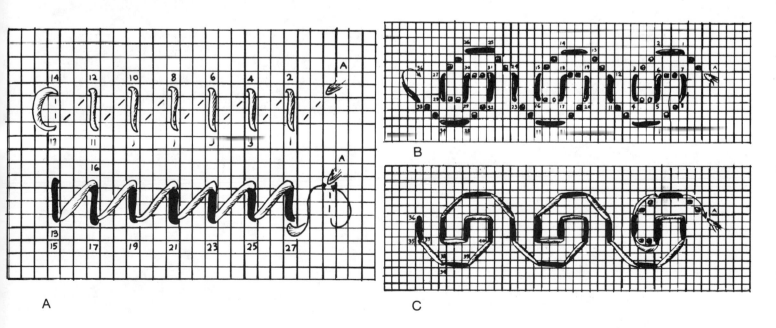

Figure 24 (A, B, & C). Diagonal and vertical sequence.

Figure 24D. Traditional Holbein patterning combining straight and slanted stitches.

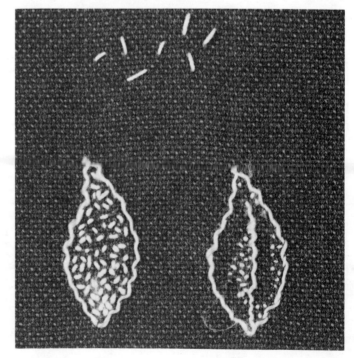

Figure 25. Seeding. Haphazard lines of running stitch as a shading technique.

Figure 26(A & B). False satin stitch. Up at 1 down at 2. Note that needle resurfaces alongside last re-entry point.

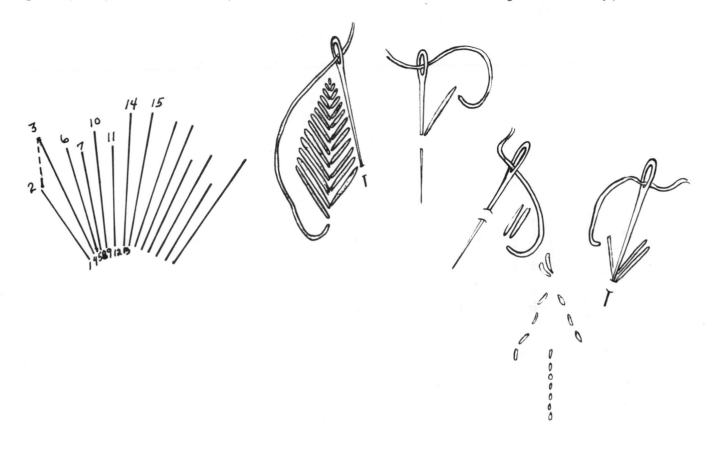

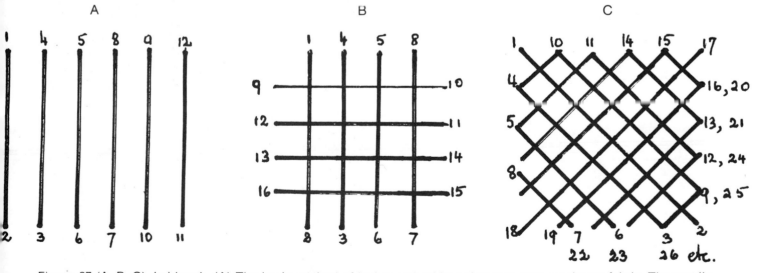

Figure 27 (A, B, C). Laidwork. (A) The basic method of laying embroidery elements onto a primary fabric. The needle must resurface alongside the previous re-entry point at all times. (B) Vertical and horizontal embroidery elements crossing one another. (C) Diagonally-laid embroidery elements.

Figure 27 (D, E). Laid threads as a supplementary background. (D) To assure flatness and to prevent overlap and cutting into the primary fabric by the needle as adjoining holes merge, remember the following: although the elements are laid parallel to one another, the space between the first adjoining set of elements must be wide enough to allow each element of the second set to fit in smoothly and to obliterate the primary fabric. (E) If several colors are used, thread the required number of needles before starting. When an adequate number of working elements have been laid, fasten the needle to the frontface in readiness for its use for the second set of laid stitches and to prevent tangles at the backface. Blend adjoining colors as shown at a, b, a, b, and c, b, c, unless a sharp color contrast is preferred.

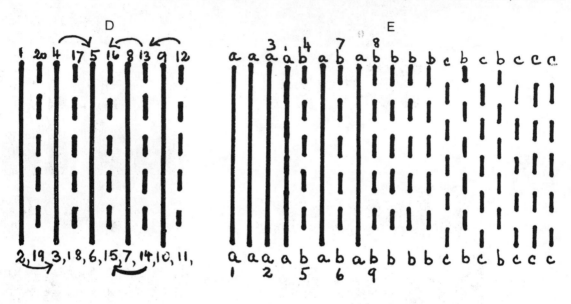

3
The Running Stitch Family and the Usefulness of Linear Stitches

A stitch functions decoratively in three main ways: to outline and define; to fill an area with solid color (or multi-color shading) and texture; or to vary the intensity of any one of the other categories by combining with other stitches. Almost any one stitch can be adapted to meet the decorating function of another by keeping in mind the relationship achieved by similarity of hand movement. A needleworker's skill, as exemplified on the Turkish textile is therefore not solely dependent upon an encyclopedic knowledge of stitch variations but rather on an ability to visualize the best method of enriching a design.

Outlining

A shape can be defined either by a strong positive outline or by a color line of interrupted stitches. An outline of strong color is the simplest and most obvious method. An outline accentuated by a wide line of stitching or by a thicker embroidery element strengthens the usual impact. A weak outline by means of unobtrusive stitching can serve as a supplement to a strong central area but used alone it decreases the importance of a shape. (*See* figure 28.)

Shapes within any motif vary, of course. Not only ovals, circles, triangles, and squares (petals, foliage, tree trunks, animals, abstracts, etc.), but also connecting links like stems and branches require a balanced definition within the overall design.

It is within this context that the value of the running stitch is most apparent, as is that of other stitches that are unrelated except for their ability to follow a line with ease by a continuous process of repetition. These *linear* stitches, despite their variety and innumerable mutations, all follow the same principles. Once a needleworker has become familiar with a few basic guidelines, the variety of his interpretations is limited only by his imagination.

To learn the different impact a stitch can have, a variety of stitches should be worked simultaneously on dissimilar fabric pieces. Stitches which depend for their uniformity of appearance on the counting of threads, as they cross warp and weft elements, will require an even-weave cloth background fabric. Non-

21

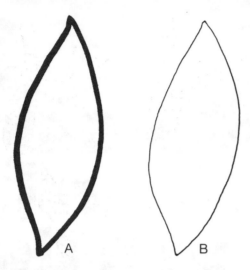

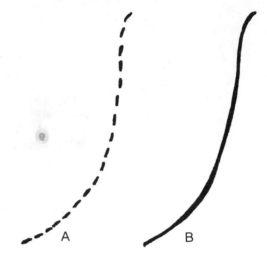

Figure 28. (A) Strong color would reinforce visibility of either a continuous or broken color line. (B) Weak color diminishes visibility.

Figure 29. (A) Broken color line (running stitches), primary fabric intrudes (weak). (B) Continuous color line as in double darning (strong).

geometric or curved design shapes will require such stitches to be adjusted accordingly. The balance of good needlework is affected by the careful manipulation of stronger, weaker, and softer stitches, and distinct patterning does not necessarily depend upon the ostentatious quality of a stitch but rather the way in which it is applied.

Use the oval form of a leaf as a practice shape; it has curves and points and is easy to draw or block out. Space, lengthen, or shorten

stitches so that the curves do not become angular accidentally. Make sure that meeting points remain sharply defined, even if you must double back on a stitch. Points or corners simply must be sharp.

Basic Guidelines

A strong color and thick element will give a positive impact, and at the other end of the scale, a light color and lightweight element will

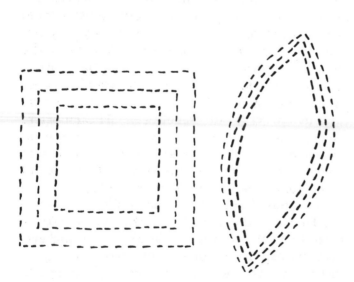

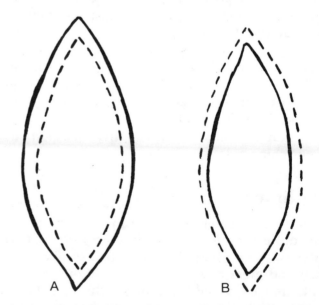

Figure 30. Multiple lines of broken color increase the width of an outline and thereby its importance. Stitches are slightly staggered to assure sharp corners and joins.

Figure 31. (A) Strong outline (color or stitch or both), soft inner line. (B) Weak outline (color or stitch or both), strong inner shape.

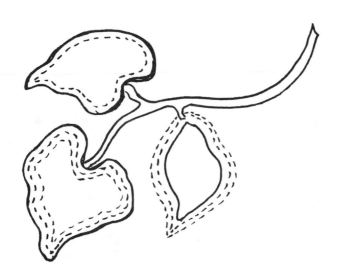

Figure 32. Stitch variations within one design.

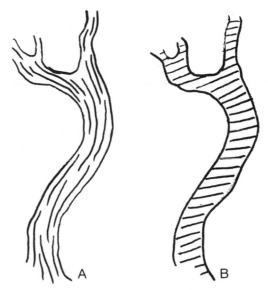

Figure 33. (A) Vertical lines increase visual impact of an elongated shape. (B) Broad lines cutting across identical shape widen its image.

minimize the effect of outlining. (*See* figure 29.) Strengthen outlines by doubling or tripling the number of rows of stitching. Watch carefully to see that outer-row stitches are either added or elongated to retain the correct shape. (*See* figure 30.)

Double darning can be used in outlining. It creates a line of solid color broken only by the shadow break. When more than one row is required, the shadow breaks can be manipulated by placing the stitch in a definite alternating, or solid sequence. Longer or additional stitches will be required for the outside row.

When you combine two different types of stitching, allowance must be made for the difference in texture. Also, you must decide whether the stronger of the two should be on the inner or outer edge. For example it is possible to obtain two different effects when the running stitch is combined with the double-darning stitch, depending on which stitch is used as the inner color. If the running stitch is used on the inside, the spaces between stitches which permit the color of the primary fabric to intrude, will result in a strong outline of double darning with a softening blur towards the center. (*See* figure 31.)

On the other hand, when the inner line is worked with double darning and the outer line with running stitches, despite their identical size, the second shape will appear smaller due to stronger, inner line of color and texture.

The needleworker can also change an outline by increasing the number of rows of one stitch or another. This would be a simple way to add variety to a standard, repeated pattern such as a spray of identical leaves. (*See* figure 32.)

Stalks and Stems

Skillful use of outlining techniques is important in working the stalks and stems of leaves. All too often, one sees gracefully embroidered flowers or foliage supported either by a single-line stitching that is too weak to support the bloom, or stitches that are layered horizontally row by row, which broadens the stem's appearance, thus detracting from the overall design. (*See* figure 33.) Stalks and stems are supportive design elements and they must flow in the direction of growth. Stylization of any one area of a design must be of deliberate intent and not a manifestation of boredom or inability.

A single line of stitching is only valid when its width is in proportion to the smaller leaves, buds, and flowers, to which it directs the eye. But instead of a single row of coarse chain—too often the easy solution in the "quickie" packaged design—two lines of more delicate stitching are more graceful and appropriate. By applying the basic guidelines for outlining, it is

Figure 34. Fruit basket. How a pattern can evolve. To prove that shading and texture do not require more than four easy stitches and that design for needlework does not require elaborate detail, the author took an old transfer printed in the 1920s and had the bowl replaced by a basket which was wider and provided more support to the fruit. Linear shading in the stem stitch was used to fill the grapes, cherries, and smooth apples. Chain stitch with its medium texture was used for the skin of the pears which is of rougher texture than that of apples. Leaves were outlined in two colors of green (alternating the shades) and left open to add a feeling of airiness. Basket in Romanian stitch but in alternating direction to shift light reflection and emphasize the interlacing with one color. Strawberries were done in shaded French knots. The omission of satin and the use of two strands of crewel were deliberate. It was the author's intention to prove that one can take a standard design and four easy basic stitches, obtain subtle shading, balance of texture, good color, and speed of work without coarseness of yarn by using two strands of a fine crewel instead of a thick hairy element. This also avoided long dust-catching stitches and enabled two shades to be threaded into the needle for the brown basket, resulting in one varying color.

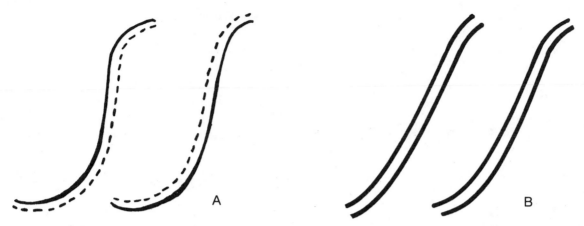

Figure 35. (A—right) Strong line emphasizes inner curve. Soft line increases width and supports stronger color. (Left) Strong line emphasizes outer curve. Soft inner curve blurs intensity of outer edge. (B) Color emphasis on outer or inner curve.

simple to see how various effects in stalks and stems can be achieved. A single line of solid color makes a more positive statement than a line with spacings because spacing weakens the effect of the line. (*See* figure 35.)

When two rows of an identical stitch are used, exact duplication of the first row by the second will emphasize the stitch's identity. But another, often more interesting effect will result by alternating the second row with the first stitch row. The addition of a stronger stitch to an outer curve emphasizes extension, or an outward flowing movement. A strong stitch within a curve seems to tighten and draw the element together. (*See* figures 34a and 34b.)

Widen stems and stalks by adding two lighter, or thinner rows, rather than a haphazard strong second line. The effect is more subtle and the gradual build up permits adjustment as the work develops since the color impact of each stitch row must also be taken into consideration. When a more stylized format is re-

quired, two definite outside rows of stitching with a softer inner core work well; or in reverse, a strong center core and two identical outside stitch lines will soften the impact. (*See* figure 36.)

An angular outline using the double-darning or double-running stitch will define geometric designs worked on an even primary fabric. One can see its effectiveness with the small stitches used to outline the Turkish design. (It is interesting to note that although this Turkish design provides an illusion of graceful curves, it is based on a methodical counting of warp and weft elements.) (*See* figure 37.) There are, however, a variety of needlework styles in which the positive shapings (the design) are not worked at all but the entire background area is covered with solid color in a stitch belonging to the thread-count family of stitches on a warp-/weft primary fabric. Assisi work (embroidery in which the geometric design is left unworked and the background is worked in cross stitch or

Figure 36. Suggested variations to increase the width of a line without double use of color or stitch.

Figure 37. Turkish silk embroidery, 16th-early 17th century. Double-darning carnations and tulips. TM 122-A. (Textile Museum pattern TM 122-A for crewel or needlepoint, based on original Turkish silk embroidery piece available.)

Courtesy of The Textile Museum

related stitches) is a well known example of this technique. To sharpen the outline of the design and to provide a clear distinction between the positive (unworked area) and the negative (worked background), the outline of the traced design is worked with the double-darning method using horizontal, vertical, and diagonal slants in a stitch size appropriate to the thread count required for the background stitch.

Counting, Stitches, and Fine Fabrics

Any stitch that depends on counting threads (either warp or weft) for its structure and patterning is difficult to use on a ground fabric so fine that warp or weft threads are not easily seen. If, as for most of us, a guideline is needed, there are several time-tested, practical methods.

Supplemental "Warp and Weft" or Framework

The simplest grid equivalent of the warp and weft interlacing is a piece of needlepoint canvas basted over the area to be worked. The canvas, whether single-thread or double-thread, should be quite thin. The only canvas to be avoided is one with a gauze weave although some of the Penelope canvases specifically woven for tent or Gobelin stitches are not suitable either as they lack an even warp-weave gauge. Stitch the design through both the primary fabric and the canvas taking care that the needle never pierces the canvas elements. In addition, the stitches must be even and taut. Use a steady up and down tug. When the work has been completed, pull away the accessory warp and weft elements with the help of a pair of tweezers. The stitches will rest on the primary fabric. (If the needle has pierced the canvas, the canvas elements won't budge, and if the stitching is loose and the canvas coarse, the stitches will look like loose little loops instead of resting smoothly on the primary fabric.)

Graph Paper

Another method is to use a sheet of graph paper, a piece of dressmaker carbon, a knitting needle, and a waterproof laundry marker with a ballpoint tip. (Do *not* use a felt tip pen.) Place carbon face down onto primary fabric and pin. Place your grid of graph paper (the size of each square should be equal to the size of your stitch) over the carbon and baste it with long stitches down the center from the top edge to the botton edge and horizontally from side to side onto the primary fabric and dressmaker carbon. Secure it at each corner. If your primary fabric has a nap and pins or basting stitches would leave a mark, pin and baste carefully at the outer edges but be sure that none of the three layers slides or begins to buckle.

With the point of your knitting needle, mark off your pattern by pressing down at the intersection of two stitch lines. A small dot will be made by the dressmaker carbon and represent the hole to be shared by two stitches. After you have finished marking the primary fabric, gently remove the graph paper and carbon and ink in the small dots with a light touch. Fragile, transparent primary fabrics are often worked by basting them onto designs that have been marked on graph paper or flexible oilcloth. In such cases, the worker, to avoid piercing the pattern, must slide the needle sideways as it enters and exits from the primary fabric. The em-

Courtesy of Dr. Elizabeth Johnston

Figure 38. Tulips. Linear shading with thin and thick stitches. Notice how the lighter colors are worked with thicker stitches and the darker lines with thinner linear stitches. Short, dark lines of Portuguese stem are used to emphasize the curving shape of the petals.

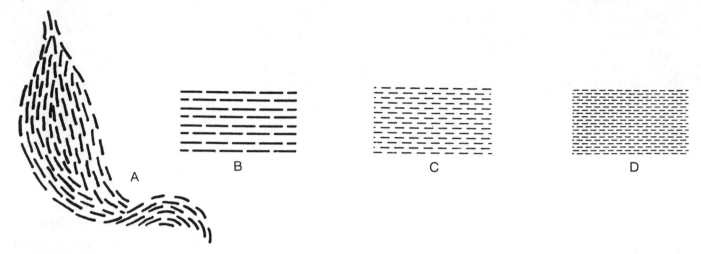

Figure 39. (A) William Morris's use of staggered lines of running stitch to fill shapes of background areas. (B) Stitches are strong and dominate area. (C) Stitches are smaller and neither background nor stitch compete for visibility. (D) Stitches dominate but have lost individuality.

broidery element will also have to be tugged and pulled sideways. Otherwise the pattern would become attached to the primary fabric. After the project is complete, the basting stitches are cut and the pattern released.

The use of supplementary tools like canvas or graph paper to enable a worker to adapt a certain technique to another environment is to a certain extent a creative challenge. It encourages refinement of skill if a previously hesitant embroiderer can work a Holbein pattern gracefully onto a silky shirt. Counted threadwork patches add humor to a favorite pair of jeans or the collar and cuffs of a work shirt. On the other hand, to spend hours counting threads to

transpose a design of counted-thread work onto even woven linen with about 24 threads to the inch is in the present day a waste of time. In this case the use of a heavier even weave would be far more practical and realistic.

A Motif with Linear Stitches

Any stitch capable of defining an outline can serve as a filling stitch. (A filling stitch indicates that an area of the primary fabric will be completely covered by stitching.) This is the primary function of many stitches. For more versatile stitches like the running stitch, and all other linear stitches, the filling status is

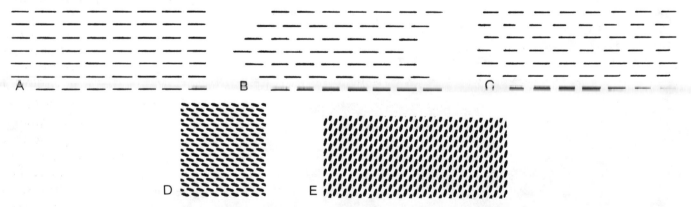

Figure 40. Shadow breaks as pattern device. The patterns created by shadow breaks—those interruptions of a smooth color-line by stitches butting against one another in a shared hole or adjoining holes—can be used to emphasize the direction of a shape if the stitch sequence of adjoining stitch lines is horizontally, vertically, or diagonally organized. (A) Horizontal lines of even-sized and even-spaced stitches are interrupted by vertical shadow breaks, vertical lines by horizontal breaks. (B & C) Staggered horizontal and vertical lines are interrupted by diagonal breaks. (D & E) By altering the direction of stitch lines the direction of the diagonal break line can be reversed (D = horizontal, E = vertical).

achieved by a constant repetition until the area is completely covered. Repetition does not have to be monotonous. The embroiderer can shift, swirl, place, and direct lines of linear stitching so that they appear as strokes of color. (*See* figure 38.)

In some pieces by William Morris, often cited as the father of England's Arts and Crafts movement in the nineteenth century, the running stitch played a dominant part in shading and emphasizing the other forms in the design. He carefully marked his designs to indicate wider spacing between running stitches in areas where he wished the background color to modify the embroidery element's color. In areas where greater intensity and shading were required, the stitches were worked close together, which gave each stitch the appearance of a thin paint stroke. The spacing between these stitches was so minimal that individual stitches seemed to be touching. (*See* figure 39.) Other linear stitches not based on the up-and-down hand movement and without spacing interruptions, can be elongated for a thinner and lighter effect, or worked closely together to emphasize or thicken their texture.

This again is an area in which the embroiderer must experiment. Not only how long or how big the individual stitch is, but also how it is placed will determine its role in the impact of the overall design. If stitches are too thick, owing to the size or weight of the element used, adjustments must be made. If too straggly and weak, smaller, closer stitches or a heavier embroidery element might be in order. The final decision must be a personal one.

Placement of Linear Rows for Filling

The effect of rows of linear stitches will differ depending on whether they are placed in straight lines, within the straight lines, within the curve of a previous row, or in swirls. Straight lines of stitching produce absolutely stylized flatness. Place rows slightly apart if a lighter effect is desired. Rows should be placed horizontally to broaden the image, but vertically to give the illusion of greater height, and diagonally to emphasize direction. (*See* figure 33.)

All lines should be worked in the same direction, or the shadow indentations or casts mentioned earlier will be uneven, and the intended visual smoothness lost. (*See* figure 40.) If the rows are stitched haphazardly as the piece of work is turned around for easier access to a certain area, the appearance of the finished area will be rougher as the direct result of the irregularity of the shadow breaks and indentations. This is an effect the embroiderer may want to achieve or avoid, depending on the nature of the piece in question.

Rows Within Rows

A more deliberate and structured use of linear shading found in Chinese and other Far Eastern embroideries is the custom of placing each line within a previous row. Start by putting the first line of stitching close to, or on top of, the outline of the shape to be filled. Each succeeding row must follow the previous line's curve or shape until the center (or core) has been reached and filled. Do not start at the center and work outward for you might discover that your continuous line of stitching is unable to conform to the outline of the shape. (*See* figure 41.)

Swirling

The third and most interesting way to use a line of stitches is by swirling them, which gives an appearance of effortless movement and life. This is not a random, haphazard play of lines. It is important to think about your approach carefully before beginning.

The simplest shading principle, which can be applied not only to linear stitches but other filling stitches as well, is to follow the direction of natural growth the shape takes. A pear, for instance, has a definite base and a pronounced stalk at the top. (*See* figure 42.) The imaginary, stitched lines of the pear in the illustration (the illustration shows only essential guidelines, not every stitch line) start at the pear's base. The first two lines of stitching follow the outer lines, one moving to the left, the other to the right, both moving towards the stalk. After the shape of the motif has been set, the inner framework lines are worked. Each line should move outward and upward, varying in length, and overlapped by each subsequent line. Actual

Figure 41. 17th-century crewel wool embroidery. Row within row linear shading for flowers and leaves. Laid work, varied French knots. Part of wall hangings formerly used at Chequers, the vacation home of the British Prime Minister. After sale, embroidery was reapplied to a new background.

stitch lines should be closely worked alongside one another, but it is quite easy to squeeze a third line between the previously worked rows, if one finds it necessary to add an additional color or texture.

Parallel lines of repetitious curving will result in a flattened, stylized shape. The natural shape can be emphasized, however, by a series of longer and shorter lines that follow the natural curve. (*See* figure 43.) As one row finishes, it is overtaken by another adjoining row begun a few stitches below the finishing point of its neighbor.

Unless the stitch direction is deliberately changed to add another dimension, it is essential to keep the flow of direction constant. When a line of stitching has reached its appropriate length, take the element to the back; either fasten it off or weave it in and out of the backside of the previous stitches until you have reached that level at which you want to bring the embroidery element back to the frontface of the primary fabric. Don't carry an embroidery element from one area to another along the back of a piece of needlework unless the distance is minimal. Long backside lines of car-

Figures 42 & 43. Linear shading of shorter and longer lines of color flowing in the direction of each individual shape.

Colorplate 2. Persia, 17th century. Embroidery—running stitch,
darning technique. "Mulham"—silk warp, cotton weft. Design illustrates
the biblical story of Potiphar's wife and Joseph (Genesis 39). TM 3.43.

Colorplate 3. (Above) Ceremonial cloth with deity figures. Peru, south coast; early Nasca style, ca. 300-200 B.C. Field—plain weave (red wool and tan cotton spun together), embroidered in double running stitch. Border—plain weave (wool), embroidered in double-faced stem stitch (wool). TM 91.205, b&w detail #B-5.

Colorplate 4. (Left) Bag with humped animal motif. Peru, south coast; late Nasca style, ca. 500-700 A.D. Warp-faced plain weave embroidered in double running stitch with cross-knit loop-stitch binding, braided handle (fragmentary), all wool yarns. TM 91.358.

Colorplate 5. Ceremonial cloth with bean motif. Peru, south coast, Nasca area, possibly Cahuachi. Early Nasca style, ca. 300-100 B.C. Field—plain weave (cotton), embroidered in stem stitch (wool). Border—cross-knit looping (wool). TM 1965.40.23.

Colorplate 6. (Opposite page, left) Tree of Life. The tree was designed by Ruth Prengel after an 18th-century Western Export textile at the Victoria and Albert Museum. Worked by Dr. Elizabeth Johnston. Colorplate 7. (Opposite, top right) Tree Trunk. Linear shading—stem stitch in longer and shorter lines (note the subtle shading). Texture—Portuguese stem stitch and double knot. By turning a piece sideways and working horizontal rows of knotted and looped surface stitches the last row can provide additional texture by remaining loose. (Detail from colorplate 6.) See figure 89 for additional information. Colorplate 8. (Opposite, bottom right) Grape Cluster. Solid cluster stitch units do not need to be heavy clumps if their individual color is shifted. Note lace stitches (alternating color rows) and soft shaded leaves. (Detail from colorplate 6.)

1968 - 1969   Elizabeth Johnston M.D.

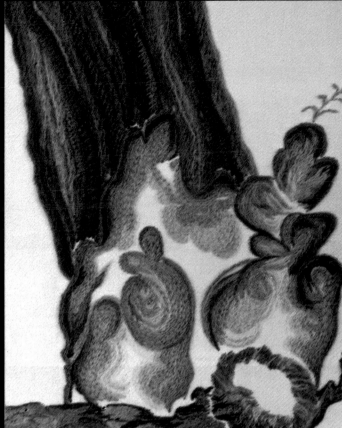

Courtesy of Dr. Elizabeth Johnston

Colorplate 9. "Love."
Machine embroidery, 1914-1918.

Colorplate 10. Mandarin square.
Ming, late 15th, early 16th
century. Bear—Military 5th Rank.
Embroidery on gauze.
TM 1970 11.5.

Colorplate 11. Canvas work, tent stitch. Blended crewel wool was threaded into needle to obtain greater subtlety in shading peaches, sky, and foreground. Worked by Mrs. Nancy Magee. Design based on a Textile Museum piece, TM 51.60B.

Colorplate 12. Canvas work, tent stitch. Leopard—outlined, no shading. Clouds— undulating shapes shaded into a soft blend, light at outer edges, deepening towards center. Any other approach would have been top- heavy in relation to the rest of the design. A leopard was the insignia of rank for a noble of the third or fourth military grade and was worn on the chest and back of the noble's robe. Beneath the leopard, a highly eroded crag juts from a sea strewn with jewels. Above are cloud forms, among which are symbols of good fortune. Satin weave, silk brocaded warp. Weft—silk gilded paper wrapped around a silk core. Worked and owned by James Parrill. Original— Mandarin square. Leopard TM 51.58. China, late 16th, early 17th century Ming Dynasty.

Colorplate 13.   A nongeometric canvas painted without fine detail will look harsh when worked in solid color blocks. The embroiderer must therefore improvise as the work develops. In this case several strands of different colored silks were blended *before* being threaded, to shade trousers and cloak details. Dragon scales were outlined with twelve strands of hair-fine silk wrapped with lurex.

Design by N. Grostate, London, after a jigsaw based on a Japanese silk embroidery at the Metropolitan Museum, New York. Worked by author.

ried embroidered elements are unintentionally pulled a little tighter by a worker and prevent the work from remaining as flat as possible.

In addition, the added dimension of effective stitch shadows should be kept in mind. Full use should be made of their effect on the design.

Choosing Stitches

A variety of linear stitches (both smooth and rough) can be worked alongside one another to fill an area in a design. A tree trunk, for instance, could have curving, vertical, overlapping lines of soft, smooth, linear stitches interrupted by the use of an odd line or two of a knotted stitch to simulate bark. (*See* figure 38 and colorplate 7.) Although an orange could be filled with a simple, knotted linear stitch, tiny knots could be alternately spaced as the lines of stitching moved upward and around to prevent the development of angular groups of knots.

Linear shading permits the simultaneous use of light or thick strokes of colored texture and must therefore be considered an important aspect of free form embroidery.

Although much of what has been said about linear stitches is directed to free form embroideries, the use and scope of linear shading can also be applied to canvas work. Although every stitch of every stitch line must emerge or reenter the canvas through one of the holes, the illusion of a rounded curve can be obtained by using the hole closest to the intended line. This requires a certain amount of overlap and gradually staggered stitches. To avoid a thickening of line, push the overlap aside with your thumb if it covers a necessary hole and release it after the stitch has been completed. It is well to remember that in all canvas embroidery, a coarse mesh will limit the ability to curve, while a finer weave will provide a far better illusion of curving. (*See* jacket of this book for an example of canvas work with rounded curves.)

Running Stitch Derivatives

Before leaving the simple running stitch and its development and influence on other stitches, its ability to shade cannot be ignored. Though its use does not result in an imperceptible diffusion of color in the true sense, the running stitch has been used in many needlework styles to intensify or fade out one range of one color or a variety of shades.

Seeding

When running stitches (or other seeding stitch units—knots, chain stitches, etc.) are small and scattered haphazardly within the motif area, the effect is called seeding, diapering, or powdering. (*See* figure 25.) Tightly clustered and worked in a random direction, the small one-color stitches will appear true to form and the tone of the primary fabric will be barely perceptible. As the worker begins to widen the distance between individual stitches, the background tone will intensify and the stitch coloring diminish. If this principle is extended to its extreme, the upper or lower area of a motif will have the deep clustered coloring of stitching, while at the other end, the color of the primary fabric will dominate. A linear stitch generally frames a motif patterned and colored in this fashion. Care must be taken that the stitch is strong enough to define the shape of the motif. Using the two basic examples of running and double darning to represent weak and strong, it can easily be seen that the running stitch intrudes on the less positive seeding arrangement, while a firm outline adds the necessary enrichment.

There is a common tendency to define seeding as the use of straight stitches as an overall filling medium. This is regrettable since there are many stitch patternings that permit an interplay between stitch, texture and background but do not, however, lend themselves to the subtleties of seeding. These are stitches with greater textural impact, and color variations can diminish or intensify their importance.

False Satin Stitch

After analyzing its structure, the false satin stitch must be placed in the family of the running stitch, despite the fact that the required hand movement may seem stilted after the easy flow required for other stitch variations. (*See*

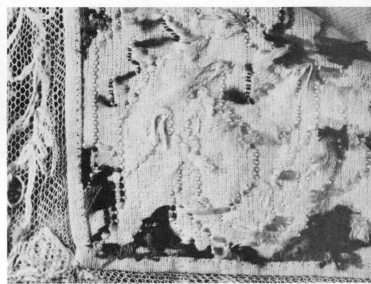

Figure 44. Many traditional Central-European folk costumes show bright silk-floss embroidered caps and overblouses of "flat stitch" work with distinct geometric shadow breaks between one area and another. They are of special interest as the embroidery simulates the slit-tapestry weave of the Kilim rugs and Chinese K'o-ssu silk tapestry technique on the frontface of the primary fabric. A simple, quick but colorful and frugal use of laid embroidered elements (false satin stitch).

figures 26a and b.) In its appearance and in its shading potential as a filling stitch, the false satin imitates the richer and fuller looking satin stitch. It is, however, flatter and nonreversible. Requiring considerably less embroidery element than other shading-stitch variations identical in frontface appearance, the false satin seems to be a stitch that owes its origin to a need for economy—a poor man's version of the luxurious. (See figures 44a and b.)

There can be no better conclusion for the use of the basic straight stitch than its ability to duplicate warp and weft elements (not to patch, but to ornament) on a primary surface. Laid threads, as they are known, provide the supplementary framework for a variety of fanciful and patterned stitch repeats used to fill a motif. (See figures 41 and 45.) These are generally known as combination stitches. Extremely popular in 17th century England during the great period of Jacobean embroidery when technique was valued more highly than design, laid threads are an extension of the false satin stitch. Straight lines of embroidery element are first laid in one direction, then crossed in the opposite. Spacing between each line must be identical and the embroidery element must be taut at all times. A hoop (or frame) to hold the primary fabric is essential. Once the lines have

been laid and a patterning of small squares or diagonals is apparent, another set of stitch structures is used either to tie down the intersections or interlace them. In addition, embroiderers took great pride in filling the spaces with additional stitch patterns for even greater elaboration.

An area can be entirely filled with a closely laid supplemental foundation, either in a solid color or slightly shaded. This permits the use of combination stitches, required to tie down the newly laid foundation in order to work with a background color other than that of the primary fabric. To key the individual long lines of embroidery element close enough to one another so that there is no risk of the primary fabric showing through, the worker just lays every alternate element and when the area has been completed, works back to the beginning by filling the missed spaces with the necessary laid line. (See figure 27d.) The introduction of more than one color is quite easy if, instead of a definite color division, color lines are permitted to overlap and thereby acquire a more subtle blend.

The most important point to remember about additional surface foundation structures is that all embroidery elements return to the frontface of the primary fabric alongside the reentry point of the previous stitch, whatever the distance in space between two stitches might be. *Never* do all correctly laid stitches come up at one side and go down at the other.

Figure 45. Satin stitch and laid stitch. Art needlework. A portion of May Curd Sampler. (*See* figure 3.)

4

Stitches Made with a Circular Hand Motion

One family of stitches dominates needlework. This family includes the universally known satin stitch and its many highly decorative variations. Their origin is unknown but the quality of the embroidered textiles found by archaeologists in the Far East, Western Hemisphere and Northern Europe indicate that their use was of long standing.

These stitches differ from the running stitch by an important change of hand movement. The new hand movement is circular, a wrapping motion which enables the stitch to envelop a fabric from both sides. Instead of a single stitch on one side of the primary fabric there are two. The stitch on the frontface of the primary fabric is the ornamental unit, its length and direction yielding to the demands of the design. The backface stitch serves as a link and is never identical in length or slant to its partner. (*See* figure 46.)

Instead of moving a row of stitches from right to left or left to right by guiding the needle up and down, down and up the needleworker must now think in terms of up-over-down-under-and-up before a second stitch can

be started. (*See* figure 47.) Necessity may have been the catalyst for this spiral of stitches. The most practical use of a circular wrapping motion in sewing is overcasting. Overcasting raw edges is a method of fabric reinforcement used by weavers to prevent fraying of all nonselvedge edges of a woven fabric. A refinement of this technique (to hide the short warp ends) was to turn the edge inward in a fold or roll before using overcast stitch variations. A variety of these techniques was identified in the Feddersen Wierde discoveries. (*See* figures 48 and 49.)

Overcasting as a purely decorative phase of needlework is known today as *whipping*. (*See* figures 50-52.)

Stem Stitch

The development of practical overcasting as a means of ornamentation has contributed a stitch of major importance to needlework. The name *stem stitch* bears little resemblance to its structure or its importance. The stitch is rooted in, and identical to, the forward-moving and

35

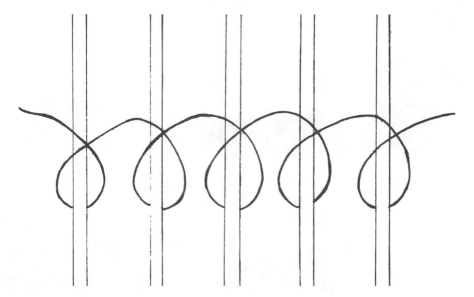

Figure 46. Progressive weft wrapping. The forward flow of the weft is broken by a backward movement which permits the weft to wrap around or surround the warp element before continuing. Soumak weave.

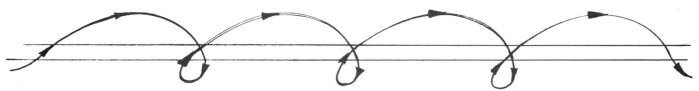

Figure 47. The embroidery element moves forward and back across the primary fabric in a series of alternating up and down movements. Front and backface stitches will be dissimilar unless the needle moves forward, down, back, up, and resurfaces at the original starting point.

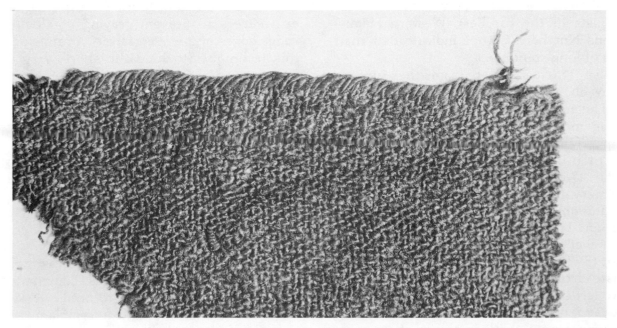

Figure 48. Double row of overcasting. "Die Textil und Lederfunde der Grabung Feddersen Wierde" by Rudolph Ullemeyer und Klaus Tidow. *Probleme der Kuestenforschung in Suedlichen Nordseeqebiet*, Vol. 10 70a-h.

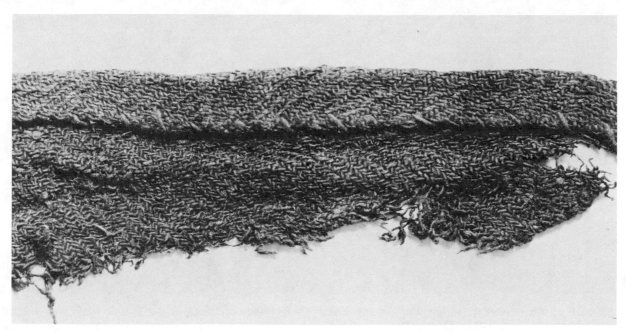

Figure 49. Overcast or "whipped" rolled hem. Feddersen Wierde. Progressive weft wrapping. The forward flow of the weft is broken by a backward movement which permits the weft to wrap around or surround the warp element before continuing. Soumak weave.

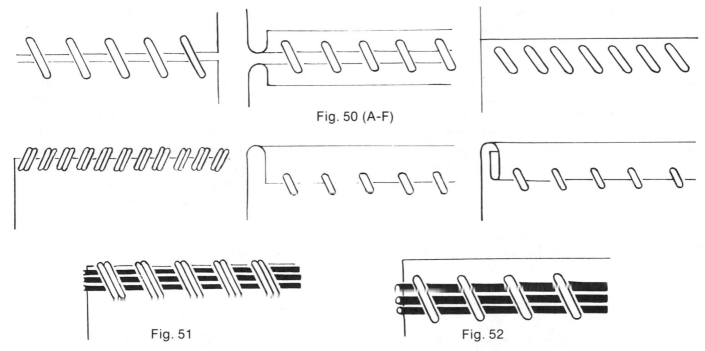

Fig. 50 (A-F)

Fig. 51

Fig. 52

Figures 50-52. Overcasting and Seaming. The following comments by Rudolph Ullemeyer and Klaus Tidow authors of "Die Textil and Lederfunde der Grabung Feddersen Wierde" (The textile and leather findings of the bog graves at F. W.) are of special interest as they relate to the use of these stitch variations along the Northernmost coastline of the European Continent. "All the standard seam joining and overcasting techniques, except for two, have been found in earlier discoveries attributed to the Bronze (1800-800 B.C.) and Iron (800 B.C.-350 A.D.) Ages. There is however no previous record of the rolled overcast edge seen in fig. 51. Although the fragment is of a uniform brown color it is difficult to understand why two sets of elements and two sets of stitches were carefully paired along this edge unless two different colors were used to justify this technique since the use of a doubled sewing element would have served the same purpose.

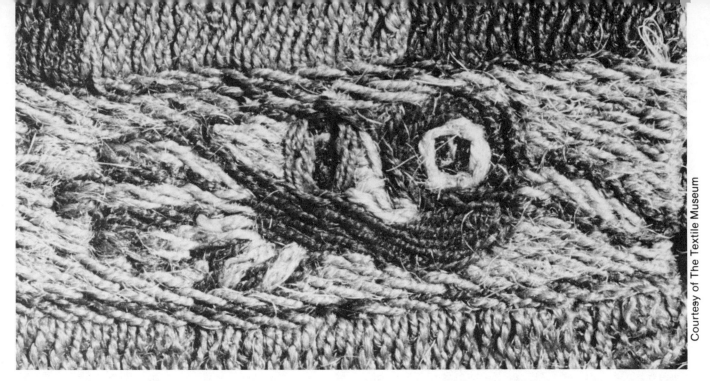

Figure 53. Detail of a border fragment. Peru, south coast. Early Nasca style, ca. 300-200 B.C. Plain weave (cotton) embroidered in stem stitch (wool). TM 91.215.

plain-wrapping weaving technique popularly known as Soumak weave. (*See* figure 46.) Working from left to right, the weaver crosses *over* two warp elements with the weft, makes a circular (clockwise) return motion which carries the weft element to the back of the warp, and by completing the circle (or "wrap") returns the weft element to the frontface by surfacing *between* the first and second warp elements. A shorthand definition would describe this action as over-two-and-under-one. If a primary fabric is substituted for the warp and the same movement applied to needle and embroidery element, the frontface will show a long stitch, the needle resurfacing halfway alongside, and a shorter, backward-moving stitch will show at the backface. When this progressive over and under, forward and back movement is repeated, a narrow line of continuous color will appear on the frontface of the primary fabric. (*See* figure 53.)

The ability to produce a line of color on the primary fabric must have been a major breakthrough in the evolution of stitches. Drawing on a fabric became a quick and simple way of introducing design and pattern. From the simple method of overcasting and forward-moving, wrapping-embroidery-stitch, the repertoire of needlework stitches would extend further and further as the basic stitches evolved into new patterns and shapes by repetition, careful spac-

ing, crossing and layering, and realignment of several individual stitches to duplicate decorative patterns found in other media.

Forming the Stem Stitch

The stem stitch is simple, but certain requirements must be met to insure evenness of repetition. After the first stitch length has been decided (shorter stitches allow better curving) and the first stitch has been placed on the frontface, the *second* stitch resurfaces at the frontface above or to the left (dependent upon whether a line of stitching is worked from left to right or upward), *halfway* alongside the first stitch. Below or to the right rests the excess loop of embroidery element, waiting to be pulled through. After the distance for the second stitch has been estimated, and the loop again swung to the right or below, the needle pierces the primary fabric for the second stitch and returns, *not* halfway alongside, but in the second or end hole of the *first* stitch. This last sequence of up-over-down-under-and-up must be repeated throughout to produce an even, smooth-plied ridge effect which is the distinguishing mark of the stem stitch. As soon as there is a slight deviation from this basic working rhythm, the stitch begins to change its appearance and sometimes its name. (*See* figures 53-55.)

Figure 54. Detail of Mantle. Peru, south coast. Early Nasca style, ca. 400-200 B.C. Plain weave embroidered in stem stitch, all wool yarns. TM 91.192.

Figure 55. Detail of a border fragment. Peru, south coast. Late Paracas or early Nasca style, ca. 500-300 B.C. Plain weave (cotton) embroidered in countered stem stitch (wool). TM 91.93.

The stem stitch has great curving potential. The curving ability of the stitch is due to the overlapping sequence of stitches which gives the illusion of a curve as the slight twist of the element hides the rigidity of each individual straight stitch. If the stitches are long, obviously the distance between each overlap is increased and the straight stitch line visible. When the stitches are short and the overlap close, the illusion of a drawn curve increases and its potential for linear shading. The stem stitch, with its extreme simplicity and solid color line is therefore a technical and creative asset, as its structure adapts itself to any imaginative challenge.

One of the finest examples of the shaping and curving possibilities of a stem stitch can be seen in a beautiful Peruvian textile in the Textile Museum collection. (*See* colorplate 5.) The motif is the shape of the bean. The colors are few and only one stitch has been used throughout. Yet, no two beans are identical. This variety has been achieved simply by shifting and changing the color combinations and the length and curve of each individual stitch row. The curved lines overlap, extend, shrink, interrupt or define, and each line is separated from its neighbor by the use of a different shade or by the shadow breaks between two adjoining rows. The stitches are minute; the primary fabric is of very fine, even weave and the stitch has been worked over-two-and-under-one.

Outline Stitch

When the excess, working-element loops are shifted to the left of the needle and stitch or above (this depends whether a line of stitching is worked upward or from left to right), the slant of the frontface overlap shifts and an upward right slant will be visible. (The other version of the stitch shows a downward right slant.) The name for this variation is outline stitch. (*See* figure 57.) A variety of changes in the surface texture of a stem stitch will change the impact of the light reflection and shadow, helping even the beginner to add variety of texture and tone to the most simple motif. (*See* colorplate 7.)

Practical Guidelines for Stem Stitch Embroidery

There are certain practical guidelines in the use of the stem stitch that one discovers either in a book or by trial and error. For instance, when using the stem stitch as shading, it is essential that all the lines of stitching flow in the same direction. This assures a smooth, layered effect and even light reflection. Haphazard back and forth stitching will produce a speckled shadow break impact that will disturb the color blend.

On the other hand, during the embroidery of a slender stalk and stem, one row of stem stitch can be worked from left to right and a second row worked close alongside from right to left with a counterclockwise movement of wrist and hand (or one row of stem and one row of outline). The result is a definite indentation between the two rows of stitching. This shadow break intensifies the sweep of the original drawn line. (*See* figure 55.)

When the consequences of a deliberate shift are seen and understood, the embroiderer can manipulate the shadow indentations and breaks to emphasize a line or a curve. The ancient artisan who produced the magnificent Peruvian stem-stitch embroidery was a master at exploiting the linear shading possibilities of the stem stitch.

Crewel

Sometimes the name of a stitch defines both a stitch and a style. Such is the crewel stitch, which is also the stem stitch. Its standard seventeenth-century variation was executed slightly differently so that the stitch had a slightly slanted appearance. (*See* figure 61.)

For centuries, crewel defined a thin, English two-ply wool spun with the best quality long staples of virgin wool (not reprocessed or short-staple fiber), strong enough to withstand the wear not only of the tug and pull of embroidery, but also of the wear of the objects.

Toward the end of the reign of Queen Elizabeth I in the early seventeenth century, the formation of the East India Trading Company began a long and dominant Far Eastern influence on English domestic fashions. The fascination with the large and bold oriental flowers, leaves, beasts, and the colors of these exotic, imported textiles produced a uniquely English decorative needlework patterning. It was a blend of new motifs with the standard practice of introducing symbolic religious, political, and sentimental emblems into a strong floral embroidery design. The resulting work was heavier and more dominant in design than before and is today known as Jacobean work. (*See* figure 41.)

In this new style of embroidery it was customary to fill all areas of the designed object with stitching and, consequently, the use of quick filling and outline techniques increased. Because wool was the most economical embroidery element and the stem stitch was in universal use, its application as a quick, flexible filling and outline stitch was practical. In due course, the workhorse crewel wool stitch and fashion became synonymous in the minds of the uninitiated, despite prolific use of other imaginative stitch combinations and variations of design style.

Back Stitch

If, instead of moving the needle up-forward-down-back-and-up in a continuous movement, one shifts direction, a different stitch will appear on the frontface of the primary fabric. Up-back-and-down-under-forward-and-up again, half a length beyond the surfacing point of the first stitch, is the first movement. During the second movement, the needle moves down to the backface at the surfacing point of the first stitch and then continues as before. This is a complete stitch reversal. The short, butted, straight stitches which used to be on the backface of the stem stitch are now on the upper frontface and the overlapping stem stitch is at the backface. (*See* figure 62.)

Known as the back stitch, this wrap stitch variation has long been used as a seaming stitch for joining two fabrics. Due to the overlap and wrapping, the stitch is too firmly embedded in the fabrics to permit easy withdrawal or separation.

The decorative aspect of the back stitch is especially valuable if the element is soft and spreads, like a silk or rayon floss. Due to the wrapping movement, the stitch acquires an additional pull and tightness absent from the running stitch. The primary fabric caught within the wrap bunches together and slightly raises the stitch. In addition, if the pull is very tight, the points of surfacing and reentry become obvious and add their shadow impact to the work. Rows of back stitching can be worked in parallel lines with the stitches aligned or staggered in a pattern sequence.

Both stem and back stitch handle more easily outside of a frame, especially for curving which requires a gradual shifting of the primary fabric. When both primary fabric and the embroidery element are flexible, the needle can enter and resurface with one movement so that the motions of up-over-down-under-and-up can be completed before the element is drawn through the primary fabric holes.

When To Use a Hoop or Frame

Needlework hoops and frames stretch the primary fabric taut and a more rigid approach to stitching is necessary. Flexibility is replaced by a regular and firm up-and-down movement of needle and wrist. Instead of a double movement and gliding, the needle is pushed down from the frontface to back by the right hand, and pushed up from backface to front by the left hand. Each individual movement requires that the embroidery element be immediately tugged and pulled in the required direction. Great care must be given to the amount of tug which each motion requires. This formal approach insures a great regularity of stitching rhythm. However, the rigidity of a previous stitch may prevent the correct resurfacing of a new one. Such is the case with stem stitch. If the embroidery element has been tugged downward to complete the last forward moving stitch, the needle will be prevented from resurfacing at its proper point without piercing the completed stitch's element. To avoid a problem, the worker must either push the element aside before the downward tug and delay the action, or with the help of the right hand thumb, push the last stitch aside so that the needle can move upward at the proper halfway mark.

The back stitch, if not required to curve, is benefitted by the use of a frame. The straight adjoining stitches can be aligned with precision and the tug can be controlled. Since the overlap is at the backface, the piercing of an embroidery element is neither visible nor is it an obstacle. One of the most practical needlework tools is a small wooden hoop varying in size between four and six inches and just big enough to stretch one area of a motif. Light enough to handle, it permits the embroiderer to shift the primary fabric for stitches based on the wrapping principle other than the stem stitch. Large needlework projects which must retain their freshness and use a large variety of stitches benefit by being stretched on a frame.

The Split Stitch

The split stitch, although identical in hand movement to the stem stitch, has no sideways overlap and is therefore narrower. It was frequently used as a very thin linear shading tool during one of the greatest medieval needlework periods. In medieval English convents and monasteries, with the help of the skilled villagers, beautiful ecclesiastical garments known as *Opus Anglicanum* were produced. They differed from their French, German, and Flemish counterparts by an embroidery style that rejected heavy and stiff ornateness.

The split stitch is never wider than the width of the embroidery element used. As the needle moves upward from back to frontface, it splits the last stitch made and moves forward by resting on top of the just-pierced stitch. The split produces an imperceptible indentation if the element is a fine wool and its quality permits the fine hairs of the wool yarn to close around the intruder. If the embroidery element is a silk floss, the indentation is more obvious. With cotton, linen, or silk, a definite separation or split will show for each stitch. When stranded cotton is used, an off-center split will show a coarse imbalance and should be avoided as a sign of poor workmanship.

The split stitch is the solution to linear stitching and shading on a frame. It is very possible that this advantage contributed to its popularity for lifelike shading of faces, bodies, hands, and feet. As the split stitch can also be found in other European embroideries and the Far East, its origin is doubtful, but there is no question about the English expertise and refinement of its use as a single, overlapping, layered line of color.

THE STEM STITCH, A MEMBER OF THE SATIN STITCH FAMILY

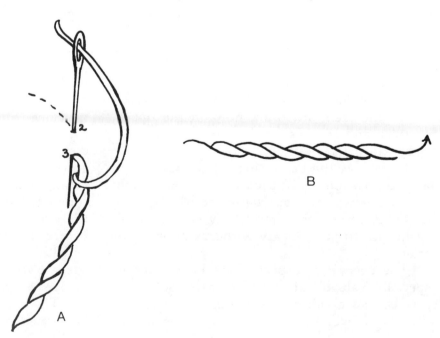

Figure 56. Basic stem stitch. Narrow width, suitable for linear shading. *Up* at all uneven numbers, *down* at all even numbers. If the stitch line is worked vertically and away from the embroiderer, the loop of the working element must be to the right of the stitch line. The slant of the overlapping stitches will resemble the *Z* direction of a twisted cord. A horizontal stitch line is worked from left to right, and the working element is below the stitch line. Overlapping stitches now slant down-to-the-right. (A) Up and loop to the right. Vertical view of a stitch row with a *Z* slant of the stitch. (B) For horizontal rows the working element hangs below the stitch and stitch slant is called down-to-the-right.

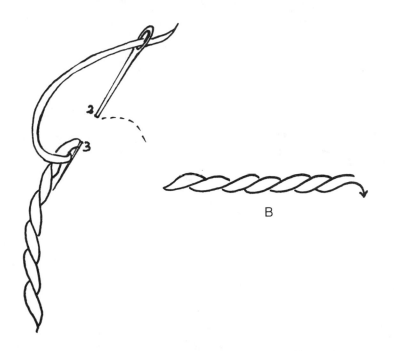

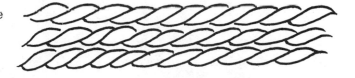

B

Figure 57. Stem stitch (outline stitch). (A) Up and loop to the left. Vertical view of a stitch row with an *S* slant. (B) For horizontal row the working loop must be above stitch line and the slant is called up-to-the-right.

Figure 58. Three lines of stem stitching running in the same up-to-the-right slant.

Figure 59. Countered stem stitch. This term applies to two successive rows of stem stitch worked in opposite slants. A distinct ridge effect will be apparent when each set of two stitch lines adjoin one another. For small stems or stalks this method will provide a tougher texture.

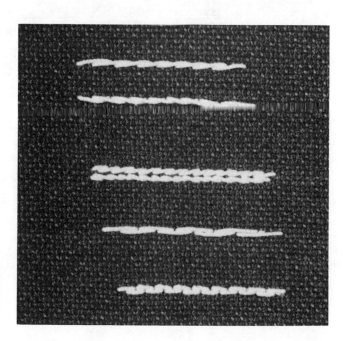

Figure 60. (A) Outline stem. (B) Stem. (C) Two lines facing one another. (D & E) Two variations of stem stitch varying the amount of primary fabric picked up by the needle.

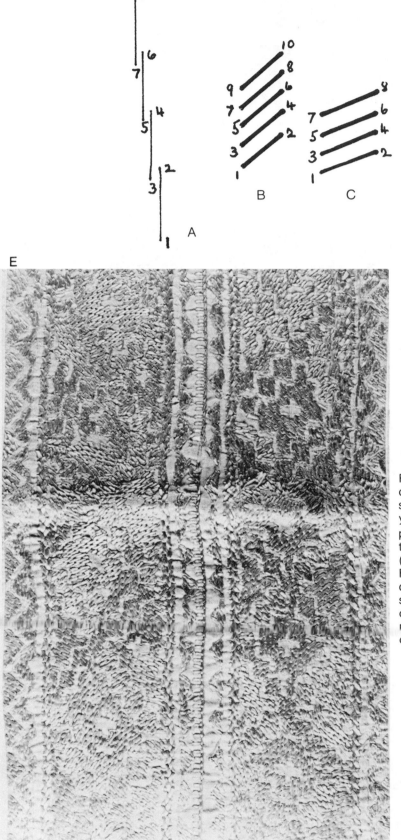
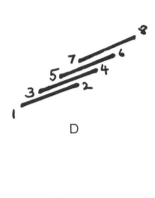
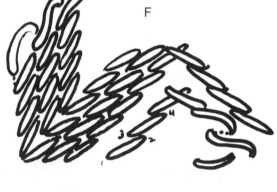

Figure 61. Slanted stem stitch, needle resurfaces *alongside* the previous stitch. Variations: the stem stitch can be elongated or widened by varying the slant and the amount of fabric a needle picks up—(A), (B), (C), and (D) show four variations. (A) Vertical stitch line, loop to the right. (B, C, & D) Horizontal stitch line, loop below. Frequently found in folk embroideries and counted-thread work. Many 19th-century Russian folk-costumes show stem stitch worked in diagonal upward-moving lines. Return movement is 1/3 of previous stitch length. Silk floss on linen. Ceremonial garment (E & F).

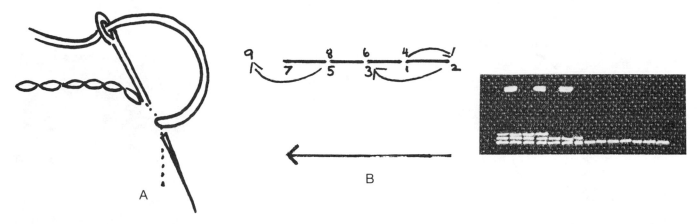

Figure 62 (A, B, & C). Backstitch (a reverse stem stitch). The soft layered-texture of the stem stitch is now at the backface of the primary fabric, while a rigid stitch similar in appearance to a running stitch now rests on the frontface. Based on the principle of up, away from the embroiderer, and down, the working element is then moved forward or towards the worker along the backface. It resurfaces at a point ahead or alongside of the original, depending upon the design and is then ready to repeat the previous movements. The personal decision of the embroiderer either to move it back to the first surfacing point or to reenter the primary fabric ahead or alongside of it will now affect the stitches' overall appearance. In the first instance, the stitches will butt against one another as they share a hole (as in double darning). If the primary fabric has a soft weave which permits its weft elements to slide, a sharp tug or pull with each forward movement will increase the size and visibility of the shared hole and add its effect to the design. The back stitch can now be considered a pull stitch. When a stitch moves back and reenters the primary fabric just ahead or alongside a small (or large) area of the background, its color will intrude onto the continuity of the stitch line. (*See* top of photo (C).) The backstitch principle is also the framework for several other stitches.

Figure 63. Double seed or dot stitch. The initial hand movements are repeated. The result is a firm, raised, straight stitch which can be used in seeding or placed in a specific design sequence.

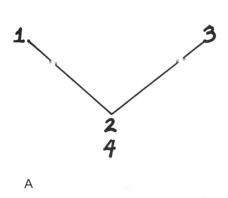

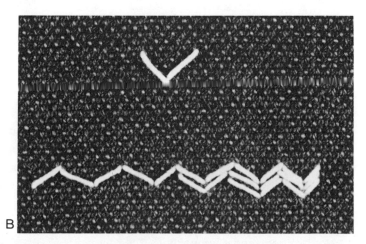

Figure 64. (A) The double seed stitch becomes an angled stitch if an extra stitch leg is added and the doubling process only relates to the second part of the stitch. (B) An angled backstitch worked with military precision and carefully arranged in vertical, horizontal, or staggered diagonal is known as the arrowhead stitch. It looks well as a diapering or seeding stitch, an edging, or as a component of a diaper pattern.

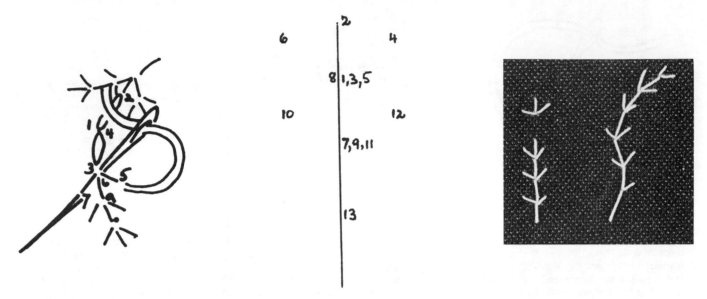

Figures 65, 66, 67. Fernstitch. A backstitch that combines straight and diagonal lines. Note that central line openings serve four different sections. If the working element is tugged too firmly a hole will become visible. It is also advisable to alternate the side at which the connecting backface stitches link one unit to another. With this sparse stitch, color must be strong enough to prevent a fade-out—unless a soft grouping of fernstitch lines is required.

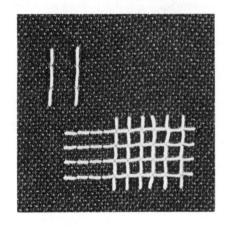

Figure 68. Back stitch trellis. Vertical, horizontal, or diagonal lines of back stitch cross and meet one another to provide a grid suitable for filling an area with a trellis pattern. Note that lines intersect at a shared opening. Due to the firmness of the stitch, the grid is precise and the intersecting lines do not need to be couched-down as in laid work.

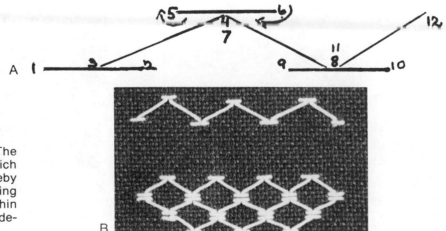

Figure 69 (A & B). The chevron stitch. The back stitch is now the framework which links two opposing diagonal lines, thereby creating a band of patterning. By working adjoining straight or diagonal lines within a shape, an overall repeat pattern will develop. Useful as an edging stitch.

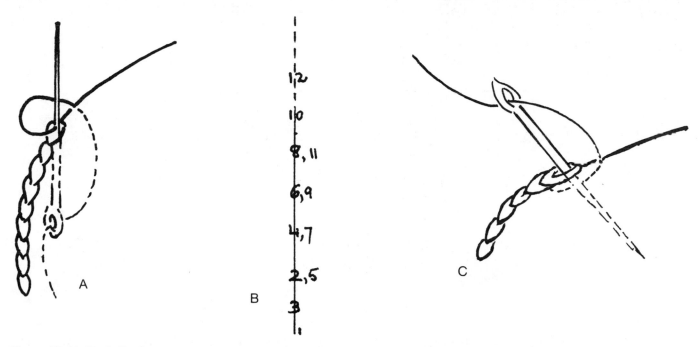

Figure 70 (A, B, & C). Split stitch. This name describes an action. The needle, instead of surfacing alongside a stitch or sharing a hole, resurfaces into a previous stitch when the split stitch moves up, forward, down, and up in the manner of a stem stitch. If the split stitch uses a reverse back-stitch technique the forward movement is along the backface—the needle moves up and then down into the previous stitch. Both methods are best worked with the material tautly stretched on a frame or in a hoop. If the embroidery element is soft and hairy the split will be less visible than if a stranded element is used. Care must be taken to pierce a previous stitch in the middle to avoid an uneven division of the embroidery element. Linear stitch, slight texture.

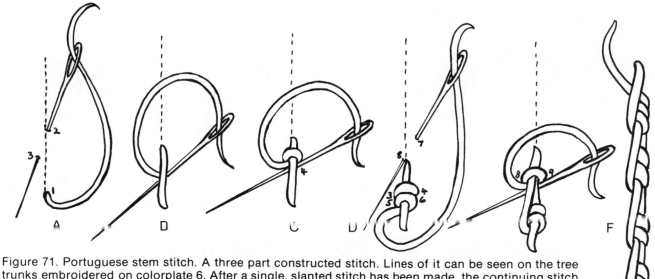

Figure 71. Portuguese stem stitch. A three part constructed stitch. Lines of it can be seen on the tree trunks embroidered on colorplate 6. After a single, slanted stitch has been made, the continuing stitch sequence is as follows: *Part I.* (A) The needle comes up to the left and center of the first stitch and instead of moving forward in a regular stem-stitch sequence, the embroidery element is moved across to 4 (B & C) and is then returned to the other side by sliding the needle between the stitch and the primary fabric. Part II. Numbers 4 & 5 (D) repeat the wrap once more (5 & 6). Part III. With the working element back at the left-hand side 5, give it a slight downward tug to tighten the two loops, though care must be taken not to straighten their curves. Move the element upward and beyond the stitch to 7 (D) where the needle reenters the primary fabric and resurfaces again at 8. Two enveloping motions now wrap not only the new stitch, but also the upper half of the previous stitch 9. Since each new stitch and the previous stitch are wrapped together, it is essential to maintain an even degree of slant for each successive overlapping stitch. A single stitch unit is completed at 7 when the element is moved to the backface. Linear stitch, heavy texture.

5

The Stitch and the Silk Trail

For thousands of years, until the practical qualities and equally lightweight weaves of synthetic fibers displaced it, silk was the epitome of luxury. Men and women wore knitted silk hose, silk shirts, silk gowns, robes, caps, and shawls. Silk was also used for hangings, and spun into threads suitable for knitting, crochet, knotting, and embroidery; and silk sheets were the equivalent of the impossible dream. The plainest country linen embellished with silk needlework became worthy of a village bride's dowry.

History of Silk

The industry started and spread out from China thousands of years ago. The old Silk Road began in Hsian (Sian) and the caravans traveled to ports in what is now Turkey, Syria, and Lebanon before their cargo was shipped to the trading centers of Italy, Spain, and Northern Europe. Each expedition involved high risks both physically and financially—to the middle men who financed the expeditions, and to the carriers and guards who crossed mountains,

valleys, streams, and deserts before reaching their final destination and such centers of Eastern spendor as Samarkand and Baghdad. Each caravan with its valuable cargo not only of silk but also of spices had to be protected against natural disasters and attack. The desire for silk by the buyer equaled the passion for gold by the seller and justified long journeys through a rugged terrain now known as the Uzbek Turkmen area of the USSR, Afghanistan, Turkey, and Iran.

Some of the best preserved and most fascinating archaeological textile discoveries have been made along the old Silk Road, in the tombs of the landowners through whose territory the caravans passed. Painted and embroidered silk from one such tomb opened not long ago in Chansha, dating from the Western Han Dynasty (206 B.C.-24 A.D.) inspired the awe of present day artisans and craftsmen.

Silk production was China's secret and no one has yet found answers to the most puzzling questions surrounding it. How did the ancient Chinese first discover that the silk filament from a cocoon that had been softened by boiling was strong and flexible, and would produce a length varying between 2000 and 3000 feet after its reelable end is found? How many hours of patient manual labor did it take to produce enough raw material for the weaver to produce one garment if the weight of a length is measured in milligrams? By what trial and error did they come upon the relationship between one type of moth which lays the larva producing eggs and the most suitable foliage for its food? The answers are not known. There has never been such a strong, pliable, luxuriously lustrous, glowing and incredibly soft weaving element as the silk thread, challenging spinners and weavers to make the coveted, shimmering fabrics. (*See* figure 72.)

Despite the textile production of wool, linen, cotton, and hemp on other continents, the desire for the secret of silk production was so great that men finally took the risk to smuggle the first cocoons and mulberry tree seeds out of China around the sixth century. Gradually silk production began in every climate conducive to the cultivation of moth and tree.

It was many years, however, before the newly developing industries could in any way match the skills of the Chinese spinner, weaver, and embroiderer. The needleworkers employed in the Imperial workshops contributed unbelievable feats of technique to the development of embroidery as an art.

Figure 72. Encroaching silk satin-stitch embroidery, 18th century. Chinese Import—Western trade. Victoria & Albert Museum Crown Copyright.

Courtesy of the Victoria and Albert Museum, London

6
Satin Stitch

The number of stitches actually used in the traditional Chinese embroideries was limited. Only after the influence of the nineteenth-century missions to China became effective and included work projects acceptable for sale in the European market, were "foreign" stitch variations included in the fabric ornamentation. Before that time the satin stitch member of the wrap stitch family played the most dominant role in free-form and geometric embroideries. It was supplemented with couching, a loop stitch, and knotting for added texture and effect.

The Chinese contributed to stitchery refinement the artistic application of those stitches that are geometrical in appearance (needlepoint) and are controlled by the carefully structured weave of the primary fabric (linen, canvas, etc.). This could be attributed to use of the cross warp weave, popularly known as gauze, which displays an open but rigid mesh and was considered one of the most desirable of Chinese silks due to its firm but diaphanous and transparent qualities. By transposing the needlework stitches used on the closely woven silks (free-form embroidery) onto the gauze as

a decorative medium, the needleworker had to focus on the easily visible spacings between warp and weft elements rather than permitting the needle to pierce the delicate fabric. This in turn regulated the stitches, each stitch being measured by and adjusted to, the number of openings used. The simplest way to describe a saton stitch is to compare its circular clockwise wrapping movement to a string which is held tight at one end by one hand, as the other hand guides it around a box until it returns along the underside and both ends meet again. Substitute primary fabric for the box, and consider the hole where the embroidery element first surfaces to the frontface as a holding hand, then carry needle and element across the primary fabric and pierce the fabric at the reentry point to the backface, and carry the element to the point where it first surfaced. A complete straight stitch (the first half of the unit) rests on the frontface and an incomplete stitch (the second half), identical in length, is ready at the backface to join with the first stitch to complete the wrap. Completion is impossible unless the needle resurfaces. The point where it ree-

Figure 73. Satin stitch. Note shadow break wherever two sets of stitches butt against one another.

merges not only completes the first stitch and completes the warp but also is the beginning of the next stitch. (*See* figure 73.)

Although at first glance the frontface view achieved by this up-across-down-back-and-up sequence looks like an ordinary simple running stitch, there is a difference. The underside stitch has two important features. It serves as a link and a slight padding for its visible mate. Instead of moving forward and following a line, each individual wrap is stationary and each frontface stitch can be compared to a penciled line. By repeating the movement, adjusting the angle of a line and its width, height, and direction, the satin stitch, by a system of block or straight-line building, can reproduce any geometric shape or fill others with color, irrespective of whether the primary fabric is of a close or an open structured weave.

The Chinese found the perfect interaction between a stitch and its embroidery element when the satin stitch was used with silk floss. Silk floss is made up of short filaments unsuita-

ble for weaving which are laid parallel to one another by a carding process, then spun, and drawn out. It is a very soft embroidery element with great manipulative and light-reflecting advantages. When used in the satin stitch, silk floss permits a blurring of stitch separation resulting in an illusion of solid color in the manner of paint. The only natural element that can duplicate the smoothness of floss, satin-stitch embroidery is a fine crewel wool.

Silk satin-stitch embroidery qualifies as one of the most effective and popular decorative needlework techniques. With the discovery of artificial silk (rayon) during the nineteenth century—a little brighter in color, a little shinier, and considerably cheaper—this style of embroidery was universal. It became associated with what was considered "lower class vulgarity".

Satin Stitch—The Controlled Wrap Stitch

Good satin-stitch embroidery requires care, pa-

Figure 74. Silk embroidered silk shawl. China, third quarter of 19th century.

Figure 75 (A). 18th-century French silk-embroidery. Long- and short-stitch leaves and buds. Back-stitch details.

tience and practice. If the stitch is done with precision and care, a viewer might get the impression that backface and frontface are identical, but in reality, the backface stitch acquires a very slight angle as the needle shifts to its correct resurfacing position beside the previously made stitch. *All* satin-stitch variations have dissimilar backface stitchlines. These add to the stitch's potential variety, as stitch rhythm can be reversed and a "wrongside stitch" used for frontface decoration. Satin-stitch reversibility was a mark of expertise in professional workshops and used for such two-sided embroidery on regimental banners. (*See* figure 74.)

How To Apply Satin Stitches

The satin stitch's main function is to fill an area and its use must be varied according to the difference in the shapes to be defined. Ribbon lines cannot be handled in the same manner as fruit and flowers, for instance. Some motifs slant towards the right and others to the left. Therefore, just as in double-darning, the form of the shape and the direction in which it moves must be considered.

The length of the stitch is another important consideration. Anything that turns the motif into a cliche and permits the satin stitch to be "caught" is too long. The dust and dirt an embroidery absorbs from the air eventually destroys the elasticity of the fiber so that long stitches begin to droop, especially if used on a wall hanging. Compact stitching of shorter length is obviously more time-consuming, but then again, neither good professional nor amateur needlework was ever produced using short cuts. Stitch length should therefore be moderate and appropriate to the design. If the shape is too large then there are two alternatives— either to select another more suitable filling stitch or to divide the shape into appropriate sections. (*See* figures 75a and b.)

The next decision relates to the slant of the stitch. When several oval-shaped leaves are attached to a stalk, should all leaves slant in the same direction despite their individual movement to the right or left? Should they all be broadened or reach upward? Would the spray have a lighter, more flexible appearance if both shapes and stitches shift to the left on one side and to the right on the other, with the top leaf

Figure 75 (B). The Myth—the backface must be as perfect as the frontface. Reality—anything goes. Professional work.

reaching upwards? The decision *must* be made by the needleworker, because every variation of slant will not only alter the impact of the shape itself but also vary the light reflection. Decisions such as these personalize the embroidery work. (*See* figure 78.) The satin stitch requires precision—sharp, clear, definite outlines. Without the adjoining holes of a structured primary fabric to serve as guidelines, satin-stitch work benefits by two previously marked lines. One upper and one lower to define the length of the stitch. The needle should surface just ahead of the line closest to the worker and enter the frontface of the primary fabric as it descends to the back, just beyond the second line. This prevents the colored marking-line from being seen, and with the stitch being worked in a direction away from the embroiderer, it is easier to gauge the point where the needle must enter or pierce the primary fabric.

Adjustments must be made when the shape is other than a straight line. Instead of starting at one side and trying to build it up, at the same time sloping the stitches in the correct slant—divide the shape in half. Very often the dividing line will cut at the widest point, and it

is easier to move from a large stitch to a smaller size than vice versa. Place your first stitch in the direction and slant you desire so that it serves as a guideline for all other stitches. Working first from the center to the left, and again from the center to the right, will produce a better stitch balance.

If a shape is quite curved, two flaws may detract from the stitch's essential smoothness. In stitching the curve, a gap may appear between two stitches along the outer, wider curve and a bunching up of stitches may occur at the lower curve or point as in the case of petals. To eliminate the gap and avoid the base-stitch cluster, leave a deliberate pie-shaped gap between two stitches at the curved outer edge and fill the gaps by the careful addition of one of two dovetailing stitches. To avoid crowding at the inner edge, don't use the same resurfacing point to begin new stitches. Instead, with your right thumb or finger, move the previous stitch gently aside and just above its surfacing point, let the new stitch emerge. The previous stitch will then cover the beginning of the new stitch less obviously. This brings up the question of whether or not a hoop or frame should be used.

Undoubtedly, the precision required by a satin stitch is more easily achieved if the primary fabric is taut.

Butted Satin Stitch

A greater test of finger skill occurs when more than one row of satin stitch is required to fill an area. Once again the needleworker has more than one option. When individual rows of satin stitch are to appear distinctive, the rows should butt against one another. However, a word of caution is in order. Generally, butting is accomplished by allowing two stitches to share the same hole. This is perfectly all right if the warp elements of the primary fabric are firm enough to be pierced by a needle and support two embroidery elements within the split. However, the combination of the cutting action of the needle and the strain of the tug and pull of two stitches might be too strong for the weave of the primary fabric and lead to a visible separation between the two rows of stitching. It is therefore wiser to leave a fraction of space between each row of satin stitch and align the stitches instead. (*See* figures 76 and 80.)

Although present-day embroiderers seldom use a primary fabric as fine as lightweight silk, the Chinese method of separating areas of satin stitch by distinct bands of primary fabric can be adapted to any type of satin-stitch work. The technique of voided outlines is exactly the reverse of the standard method of drawing or stamping the design on the primary fabric and then carefully hiding it beneath the stitching. This time, the areas to be filled with satin stitch are carefully separated from one another by a small, narrow, unworked space. Voided outlines require careful draftsmanship and very precise stitching for each section. Simple shapes like leaves and petals lend themselves well to this approach, which is, despite the extra effort, most rewarding as the colored motifs appear to float on the primary fabric. (*See* figures 81a and b.)

Encroaching Satin Stitch

A sharp division between two areas of satin stitch is not necessarily desirable in every design. A softening or blurring of the division is easily achieved by the use of the encroaching satin stitch. The stitches of the second area surface between and just below the outer edge of the first area. Instead of a cutting line, the two areas seem to merge. It is essential to see that the line of encroaching stitches is even and that no stitch irregularities disturb the first area. When shapes and motifs are more complex—flowers with reversing petals or animal shapes—it is important to remember that the slant of the stitches will influence the final appearance and that inevitably a few small or half stitches will have to be added to the curved or pointed section to help the longer and more dominant stitches to conform. (*See* figures 77 and 82.)

There are several means to attain even greater relief, in any embroidery style, than just by using the satin stitch alone. For instance, the outline of a shape can be covered with a row of running stitches and the satin stitch then worked over and across this line; the outer edges of the stitch will then be firm and slightly raised. Or the entire inner area of the motif can be covered with lines of short running stitches before being covered by a satin stitch to make the embroidered areas raised but flat-topped. (*See* figures 83a and b.)

For a stronger three-dimensional sculptured appearance, a layer of padding is worked first. An embroidery element of coarser and softer texture than the outside stitching element should be used and a needle with an eye large enough to pull the padding from the backface to the frontface without damage to the primary fabric must be used. The long padding stitches are *laid* in the opposite direction needed by the shape. The laid stitches can be arranged flat and close to one another or additional stitches superimposed across the center to heighten the area. If a soft batting element is unavailable, use several layers of a lighter weight cotton element. Each additional layer must be slanted in a direction opposite to the previous one. With the padding in place, the satin stitch is worked in the normal manner.

Figure 76. Frontface of shawl. (*See* figure 74.) Butted satin stitch at wing and back; long and short stitch shading at head and breast. Encroaching satin stitch for flowers.

Figure 77. Backface of shawl.

THE FAMILY OF SATIN STITCHES

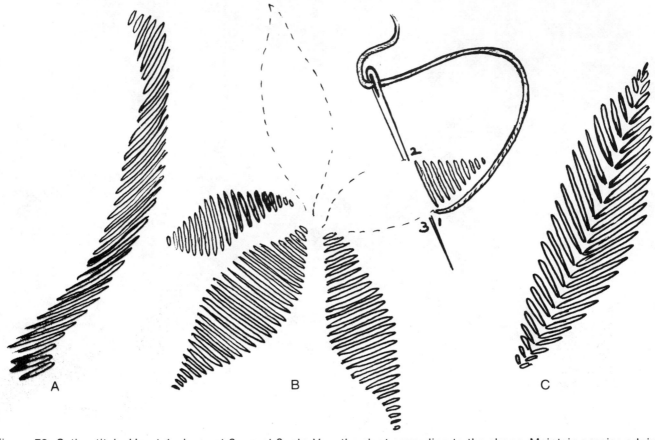

Figure 78. Satin stitch. Up at 1, down at 2, up at 3, etc. Vary the slant according to the shape. Maintain precise edging.

Figure 79. Satin stitch. Varying stitch length.

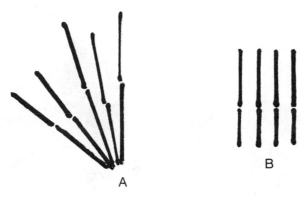

Figure 80. (A) Butted satin stitch (irregular stitch length). (B) Butted satin stitch (even stitch length).

Figure 81. Satin stitch. Block shading and void separation.

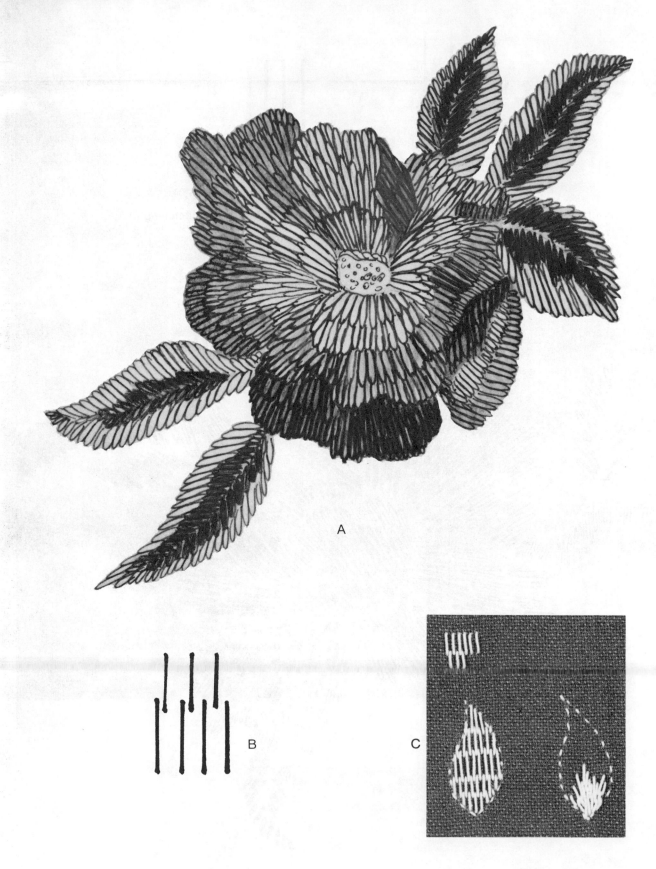

Figure 82 (A, B, & C). Encroaching satin stitch.

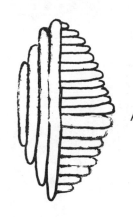
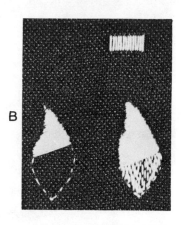

Figure 83 (A & B). Padded satin stitch. To increase the importance of a satin stitch, the stitch is first padded and then worked in the usual manner. There are two forms of stitch padding: (1) A series of running stitches are worked within the motif and then covered. The result is a higher satin stitch than previously when the stitch was worked and placed directly onto the primary fabric. (2) Additional height is added or the importance of the stitch increased when a series of satin stitches of a softer working element are first placed in an opposite direction to the final satin stitch and then completed by the second layer.

Opus Plumarium, or The Long and Short Stitch

The long and short stitch must have been a miracle stitch when it first made its appearance in the West. With it, the artistic needleworker could introduce color and texture and thus give life to flowers, figures, animals, trees, and clouds. Its Latin name, *opus plumarium*, (feather stitch) not only proves its early origins but also its importance as a prized decorative textile medium. And even towards the end of the seventeenth century and the beginning of the eighteenth, the stitch was still important enough to have retained its Latin definition. The long and short stitch is, above all, a flexible satin stitch that has great creative potential. It is not a stitch rigidly structured with precise and identical rows of long and half-size short stitches butting against one another in alternate sequence. Instead the stitch is completely controlled by the worker who selects its length and slant deliberately for a certain quality in a certain area. The key to its successful use lies in having a good eye for the direction in which the stitches should flow. (*See* colorplate 6.)

The individual stitches can best be described as straight, but each one is either longer or shorter than its predecessor. No two neighboring stitches should finish at the same level; stitch rows do not butt against one another, rather the stitches of one row encroach deeply into the previously stitched row. Each stitch surfaces to the frontface or enters the backface between two stitches by cutting into another stitch or by overlapping if needed.

The secret of a good long and short stitch lies not in its uniformity but in a programmed and spontaneous fusion of each row of stitching. Essentially a shading stitch, the object is to arrive at a beautiful flow of color with various shades blending into one another.

During the seventeenth century, English embroiderers working with crewel wools, filled their bold Jacobean patternings with monochromatic shadings of indigo blue and green using the *opus plumarium* stitch. The long and short stitch was also used with silk to shade the faces and flowers on embroidered bookbindings. Its use as a silk embroidery stitch became more widespread as the fashions of the past—the ponderous, overly ornate and ostentatious—were rejected for more subtle and natural effects. (*See* figures 84, 85, and 86.)

By the end of the seventeenth century, England's East India Trading Company regularly sent shipments of ready-cut and patterned silks to their overseas trading stations to be embroidered with long and short stitch by the highly skilled and considerably less expensive Far Eastern native labor. With the French court setting the trend, and silk the principal fabric for woven and embroidered apparel, a passion for chinoiserie began to replace the cumber-

Figure 84. (Above) Crewel, wool embroidery. Detail Chequer hanging, late 17th century. Shading—long and short stitch. Seeding—French knot. Figure 85. (Below) Detail Chequer hanging. Stem-stitch stalks, French-knot pods, long and short stitch foliage.

Figure 86. (Above) Detail Chequer hanging. Long and short stitch. Note brick stitch variation in tree trunk. Figure 87. (Below) Silk hanging. Early 18th century. Long and short stitch. Similar motifs are found in earlier wool embroideries. Possibly a Western Trade Textile.

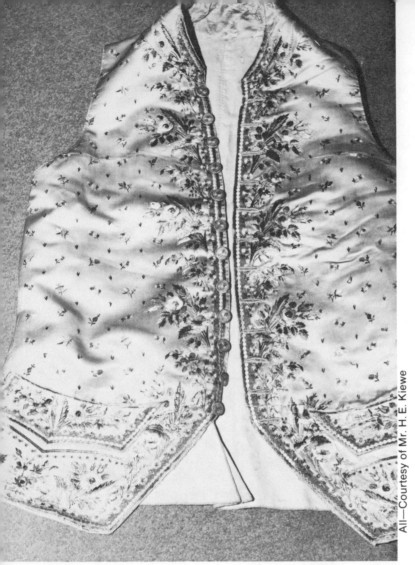

some Jacobean fusion of East and West. The elegant and simple replaced the old, and the aristocracy in all countries commissioned embroidered silk wall-hangings (wallpaper) of *opus plumarium* in lieu of the earlier imported painted cottons. (*See* figure 87.)

During the Age of Enlightenment in the eighteenth century, it was not surprising that embroidered works were more natural and realistic looking than before. With the hand embroidery of skilled needle artists appearing not only at court but also in professional workshops, and with cottage industries meeting the increasing demand for embroidered yardage for fashionable upholstery and drapery fabrics to decorate the new high-ceilinged houses with tall windows, the use of the long and short stitch and its paint-like quality gradually replaced every other stitch in popularity and fashion. By the beginning of the nineteenth century, the city of Lyon alone had several thousand women hand-embroidering waistcoats (vests) and other apparel. (*See* figures 88a, b, and c.)

The increasing use of machinery to duplicate other handmade objects of everyday life began to interest the owners of professional

Figure 88. (A—top left) 18th-century silk-embroidered waistcoat. Long and short stitch, satin stitch. (B—bottom left) Note handmade buttons and lace insertions. (C—bottom right) The backface of the waistcoat is not as perfect as the frontface. Professional work.

embroidery workshops and spinning mills as a means of increasing their own production and profit. In 1828, Joshua Heilman of Mulhouse in Alsace-Lorraine, with the help of double-pointed needles, finally succeeded in developing a machine which, when hand-guided, could embroider several flower sprigs simultaneously, emulating the feather stitch in the necessary long and short manner so well. It would take several more years of financial disasters, commercial pirating of improvements, and skirmishes between workshop owners anxious to install the machinery and workers fearing displacement, before the machine would prove capable of meeting artistic demands and demonstrate its commercial success by embroidering with hitherto unknown speed, yards and yards of *opus plumarium* embroidered fabric. (*See* colorplate 9.)

The long and short stitch must be considered a victim of the Industrial Revolution. As early as the 1860s, Queen Victoria's embroideress deplored the current lack of expertise. In an age when needlework was part of every girl's curriculum, the appeal of the new and mass produced embroidery books and magazines lay in their use as supplemental dictionaries and guidebooks for pattern inspiration. Eventually the obvious was described in technical language and the knowledge of a stitch's creative use was taken for granted. Unfortunately this profusion of standardized texts and drawings became the first step towards mechanical hand embroidery and contributed to the deterioration of embroidery as a creative craft form.

A hundred years later the long and short stitch was considered to be time-consuming, difficult, and an extravagant embroidery technique; it was replaced by large chunks of solid-color satin stitch in mass-produced embroidery kits. Consumer analysis has indicated that the twentieth-century woman looks for quick results first. Occasionally a kit based on a museum piece with a long and short stitch design reaches the marketplace, but in the transition from original to copy, the kit is seldom kind to this beautiful stitch.

Practicing the Long and Short Stitch

It is easier for a beginner to work the first set of long and short stitches on a practice piece without the benefit of a hoop. By shifting the hand-held primary fabric in various directions to find the best angle from which to make each stitch, the novice learns greater flexibility. With greater confidence, the use of a hoop or frame is recommended to stretch the primary fabric. Stitches will be more even and the embroiderer gets a better overall view of the motif. For smaller projects, a hand-held small hoop, 4" or 6" in diameter is quite practical and easily shifted. For large designs, a floorstand hoop or frame leaves both hands free to stitch. The left hand to push the needle upward and the right to push it down. In professional workshops, embroiderers have always been seated around large floor frames and this may well be the reason why the long and short stitch is often diagrammed as being worked from the outer edge of the motif towards the needleworker. Each worker undoubtedly found it easiest to work the furthest areas first, the nearby, last. It would also have kept the work cleaner, and prevented rubbing and thereby fraying a previously worked area.

Since each long and short stitch is placed individually within a motif, a stamped or drawn outline is essential for anyone who is not quite sure of how a shape is formed or how colors blend. Seed catalogs, as well as the pictures in *The National Geographic* provide excellent guidelines for fruits and flowers. The clear, sharp photographs define the direction and shading of every vein and thus help the needleworker who will discover that no flower is ever composed of a single color. To reproduce animals and their muscular structures by shading in needlework, good black and white photos are more helpful than colored. Their stronger contrasts provide more obvious directional guidelines.

Check the direction of each area of a motif to be worked *before* you start stitching. The veining of petals usually fans out from an outward moving base point; a bird's feathers move down the neck and not upward, and so forth. (*See* figure 89.)

Figure 89. Butterfly detail from shawl (figure 74). Texture achieved by use of long and short stitch, satin stitch, back stitch.

Start by finding the bottom center point of a straightlined area to be worked and bring your needle with the colored embroidery element up from backface to frontface. Your first stitch is now ready to move forward and down. Decide in which direction it should point, consider the longest length you require, and return it to the backface. Tug and pull the entire embroidery element to the back so that the first stitch is anchored and flat on the frontface of the primary fabric. Never at any time feel tempted to resurface the needle for the second stitch, however sure you are of the next surfacing point, before completing the previous stitch. With one stitch complete, place the next stitch alongside either to the left or to the right of the first stitch. The second stitch must either be *shorter* and therefore *lower* than the first stitch or even *longer* and *higher*. Continue in this manner until the first half of the line has been completed. Return to the center and work from the center to the opposite side in the same manner. The next row and every succeeding one is worked with the same rhythm of shorter and longer stitches, judging the distance and necessary slant best suited to the overall shape and gradually building up the entire area— remembering that each stitch is always either shorter or longer than its predecessor and that stitches are only level at a base or outer edge. Since every motif or detail varies in shape, it helps to think of the stitches as straight lines of irregular length which are placed side by side.

For greater subtlety of shading, stitches can come up between previous stitches, underneath a previous stitch by pushing it aside for a second and then releasing it, or into a stitch already worked. If stitches must give an illusion of curving outward or inward (straight stitches cannot be curved) smaller stitches must be layered and overlap one another in a forward moving direction. The stitches might then resemble a stem stitch but their texture is different. Once the intended sweep is accomplished, the longer stitches can again continue to move forward. Avoid tiny, cramped stitches except at an inner curve and make the first, directional center-stitch long enough to indicate the sweep of the stitches. Wool and floss will not show the split of a needle surfacing into a previous stitch, but corded and stranded embroidery elements will show the split. In that case, use the camouflage of a previous stitch to hide the beginning of another. All outside edges must be sharp as those of the satin stitch.

Written instructions generally tend to give an impression of a major undertaking. But the long and short stitch is really quite easy if you permit yourself to break the rules sometimes associated with it. Speed in working comes with confidence in stitch placement and color. Color can range from dark to light or light to dark. More than one shade of one color or several different colors can be used. Sometimes a petal might require two half circles of a strong color framed by background shades. In such a case, work the half circle first with short, layered stitches and then begin to adapt the other stitches to fit into the remaining area. If your first attempts produce a few visible bare spaces of background primary fabric, simply insert an extra stitch longer or shorter than its neighbors. In the same manner, you can remedy any consecutive rows of longer and shorter stitches that don't seem to fit into one another.

The long and short stitch is a very flexible stitch and can be used on a needlepoint canvas as well as on closely woven primary fabrics. It adapts itself like the linear stem stitch to canvas by surfacing at the closest hole under another stitch which has been shunted aside and then falls back into place.

THE FAMILY OF LONG AND SHORT STITCHES

Figure 90. Long and short stitch (shading).

Figure 91. Long and short stitch (blending color and shape).

Figure 92. Long and short stitch (blending color and shape).

Figure 93. Long and short stitch. (A) Up at 1, down at 2, each succeeding stitch longer or shorter than the previous one. (B) Second row must encroach into previous one.

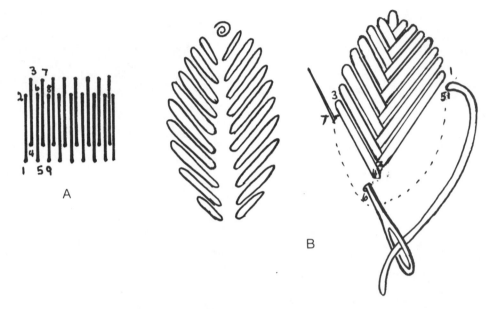

Figure 94. Flat stitch variations based on satin stitch. There exist a number of wrapping motion stitches which are flatter in appearance than the standard satin-stitch variations. Their structure is not based on a simple up, across, down, back, and up. But instead—up, partially across, down, partially back, and then up again. The stitch is then worked in a reverse sequence and moved back to the other side. By increasing the length of the visible frontface stitch and thereby decreasing the length of the backface stitch, the double-element layer essential to all satin stitches disappears and instead is replaced by a more economical wrapping system. The most simple of these substitutions worked in horizontal lines is the New England flat stitch. Found in colonial crewel embroidery, it probably served as a thread saving substitute for the more extravagant long and short stitch customary in the old country. The backfaces of old English crewel pieces do, however, indicate that simultaneous use of both shading techniques within one area was not uncommon and is evidence that settlers were familiar with "thrift" stitches. (A) Horizontal flat stitch-line (vertical stitch). Worked from left to right, the basic flat stitch must not be confused with a false satin stitch which has different hand motions. This is not a stitch where the needle is pulled up and down, but rather, it is moved in a gliding sequence more reminiscent of a figure eight. Coming up at #1 the needle is moved towards #2, reenters the primary fabric and immediately resurfaces at #3. At that point, needle and element are pulled forward and out and the needle returns to the primary fabric at #4, resurfaces at #5, and is pulled towards the worker. By varying the amount of fabric which the needle picks up as it moves from one stitch to another, adjoining stitch lines either butt against one another (minimal amounts) or encroach deeply. Thanks to the flexibility of an embroidery element, close adjoining stitches will appear as long and short stitches, their true working identity only apparent at the back surface which shows the short linking stitches. This is a filler stitch with flat texture. As soon as the slant or working direction of the stitch or stitches is changed, but the same technique applied, the difference in pull and tug and placement will alter the appearance of the stitch. Horizontal stitches, pulled sideways will result in a vertical, flat stitch-line and vertical shadow breaks between two and more adjoining lines. When the slant is diagonal an entirely different pattern-system can be developed as each alternating stitch moves beyond the previous one but does not cross it. By adjusting the stitch angle, shape illusion can be broadened or narrowed as seen in the fishbone stitch variation while its use as a filler stitch is easy and quick. (B) Fishbone variation, backface and frontface.

Chinese Embroidery on Gauze

Chinese satin stitch embroidery on gauze, like any other canvas embroidery, appears geometric in the process of interpreting a design. Upon closer examination, curves on the fine gauze primary fabric are stepped horizontal or vertical lines. A beautiful example of this type of embroidery technique is the Mandarin Square in the Textile Museum, Washington D. C. (*See* colorplate 10.)

Colors are few and the size of the stitch varies as does the grouping. The use of the satin stitch throughout as a covering of the primary fabric rather than as an accent stitch now changes its appearance. The repetition of the shadow break, wherever two stitches butt against one another in a common hole, adds an overall pattern to the design. Just as in Florentine work, the flatness of the stitch is broken up by the carefully modulated variation of

Figure. 95. Florentine embroidery on an even-weave primary fabric, when at its best and in the classical patterning of the Renaissance, provides the illusion of color floating in space. These two patterns were charted by Mr. H. E. Kiewe during the 1930s from authenticated silk-embroidered Florentine pieces.

stitch length and grouping as the deeper color tone of the break adds a third dimension to the overall image and varies the reflection.

One of the easiest, most relaxing, and most pleasurable forms of canvas-work is Florentine or Bargello due to its liberal use of color and flowing, undulating lines. (*See* figures 95 and 128.) Predominantly used as a wall covering, coverlet, hanging, or upholstery material during the Renaissance, it can be worked with soft silks on a fine canvas to produce a smooth, glowing, and elegant work. On the other hand, the same pattern worked on a coarse canvas, with heavy yarn and bright, bold colors is compatible with rural embroideries or bold contemporary furniture. Florentine is worked exclusively with the satin stitch on canvas, the difference between one pattern and another being dependent upon the variations of stitch placement—single stitches or groups of stitches being staggered in a set sequence.

Bargello refers to a famous museum in Florence that was formerly a palace. It now houses some of the most important remaining samples of this popular Renaissance canvas-work fashion. Florentine defines its origin: the city of Florence, the center of commerce to which bankers and silk merchants returned after trading in every major European city. Bargello or Florentine has yet a third name, Hungarian flame stitch, which implies but does not prove that the embroidery originated in Central Europe.

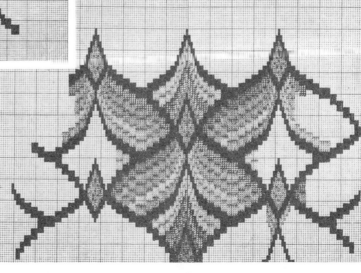

Figure 96. 19th-century petit-point canvas embroidery. Forty stitches to the inch. French, silk canvas-threads. (Author's collection.)

Since Florence was one of the most important silk producing centers, it had direct trading contact with the Near and the Far East. It is therefore likely that this style of needlework might not be exclusively a European creation but rather the development or extension of the use of the satin stitch by Chinese embroiderers. They plied their needles to depict rivers and ocean waves crashing against rocks with the satin stitch on gauze primary fabric. An experienced and interested worker could easily effect changes by varying the staggered up-and-down placement of the individual stitches, changing their length and exploiting the rich color ranges common to silk. The name *flame stitch* is thus justified. The most beautiful of these embroidered fabrics had greater body than a woven silk. With their shadow and light variations, they projected luxury and richness and were used both in ecclesiastical and secular environments.

However intricate a Florentine stitch sequence might appear, once a certain horizontal line has been set, every additional row is simply a repetition of the previous one. Only the colors change. Once an interlocking, curved motif is completed, every other additional motif is linked to it. It was only necessary that the experienced professional "set" the pattern, and issue the necessary color instructions. The apprentices completed the work. Florentine work was not only beautiful and simple, it also had a commercial advantage. If the same patterns had been woven by hand (before the invention of the Jacquard loom), the undulating intricacies of the flaming peaks would have required the services not only of a master weaver but also of a drawboy, whose job it was to raise the necessary loom heddles through which weft elements have to pass.

The Florentine style was also very popular in England. Trade between English and Italian merchants was of long duration. Since the use of wool was as common in England as that of silk in Florence, it is not surprising that seventeenth century wool merchants substituted wool for silk and used Florentine embroidery as an insulating wall covering. It was less elaborate but not as expensive as tapestries.

Florentine patterns were also collected, varied, and used extensively as upholstery materials for wing chairs. This fashion was transferred to eighteenth century Colonial America and was not just used for furnishing but for billfolds, slippers, needlecases, and the like.

The Satin Stitch on Canvas (Needlepoint)

Of the numerous slanted satin stitch variations on canvas, the tent stitch (sometimes known as stroke stitch, tapestry, or gobelin) with its one left-to-right slant, and its numerous relatives must be considered the most common. It provides a soldierly alignment of stitches with the very first stitch establishing height and slant and all other stitches following suit. As the rows begin to build up, the finished work assumes a mosaic quality with the small shadow breaks marking the separation of adjoining stitches. (*See* figure 98.) The popularity of the tent stitch as a wool-working slanted satin stitch on canvas began when people realized that the stitch could give a considerably cheaper domestic version of the highly prized Flemish wool tapestries. Once again the purpose was to duplicate a woven look. (*See* figure 96.)

Flemish weavers used fine linen warp elements which were closely spaced. As the earlier mentioned alternating rows of weft were beaten down for extra firmness and to cover the warp, all weft picks lying on the raised warp elements were pushed upward to the frontface, while the alternate weft elements were pushed against one another at the backface. As a consequence, the close adjoining weft picks had the appearance of short horizontal satin stitches butting against one another. Horizontal lines do not lend themselves well to the subtle shading which is the essence of the great medieval art of tapestry weaving. The handicap was resolved by turning the design sideways, weaving the shading details known as hatching in the usual horizontal manner and, once the work was completed and cut off the loom, returning the work to the original position of the design. The short weft picks would appear now as slightly slanted vertical lines. The apparent slant was due to the light impact of the raised texture on the double layer of the weave.

Curiously, many old pieces of tent-stitch tapestry embroidery do not show the stitch worked in the standard left to right sequence until the work is turned sideways. It is possible that early professional tapestry embroiderers used the same technique as the weavers reproducing a design from a side view in the belief that greater subtlety could be achieved. Actually the only difference seems to be that the stitch angle runs from right to left.

With the invention of Penelope machine-woven interlaced canvas in the early 1800s (similar to gauze), which prevented the sliding of warp and weft elements during embroidery, the worker could double the number of "holes" available for stitching by pushing the close parallel weaving elements apart. This discovery enabled workers to use two different sizes of tent stitch within one piece—the gros point (large stitch) and the petit point (small stitch). As demand increased, the latter became finer and finer until finally, entire pieces were worked in petit point, generally ranging from 20 to 40 stitches per inch. The latter are worked on hair-like gauze with a magnifying lense. (*See* figure 97.)

In canvas work, (known as needlepoint in the United States but tapestry or gobelin embroidery in other parts of the world) there is no interplay between the stitching and the primary fabric as a background; rather the stitching is both background and design. This stitch system is a deliberate attempt to duplicate the more costly and time-consuming aspects of weaving. To understand this fully, a more detailed explanation of tapestry weaving is required.

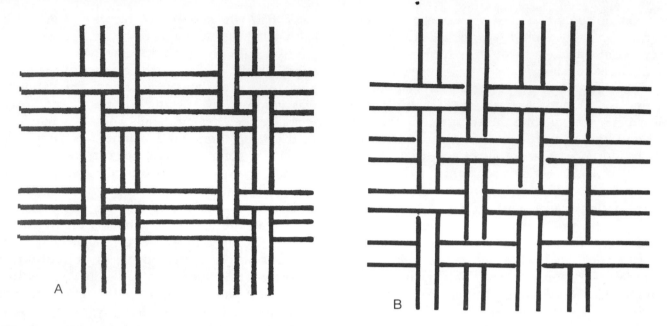

Figure 97. Penelope canvas. (A) Double mesh. (B) "Split", single (uni) mesh, to make petit point.

Only the most skilled weavers were employed to copy the original designs or cartoons drawn by the famous painters and masters of medieval Europe due to the artistic and technically precise work required. After the weaver has stretched a set of warp elements and interlaced the first colored weft element through them, only a broken line of color will appear (*See* running stitch). In order to achieve a solid line of color, the worker returns to the starting point by inserting a second colored weft along the alternating shed. This row crosses the previously visible warp elements (*see* double darning) and thereby achieves the desired effect. This technique when used to reproduce detailed objects instead of repetitive patterns was slow and time consuming.

In canvas work, a basic slanted satin stitch known as tent stitch—crossing one warp and weft interlacing of the canvas—is used to duplicate the weaving technique. (*See* figure 98.) The overcasting, circular hand movement of the satin stitch, covering a stiffened open warp-/weft primary fabric (canvas) framework imitates the colored weft pick or shot. The need to cover the entire surface and hide the canvas framework can, despite its soothing qualities, become tediously repetitive unless the design is interesting. An even, steady rhythm of pull and tug must be maintained since the overall smoothness (if only one stitch type is used) is essential in canvas work. A second stitch should never be started before the first one is complete and the embroidery element pulled down to the backface—especially if the design requires careful shading. In addition, one must observe the mathematical sequence unique to each variation of the basic straight or diagonal satin wrapstitch in order to be sure the primary fabric will be covered.

Every visible hole will be used by two stitches unless the primary fabric is to be shown for effect. The stitch which surfaces from a hole (the up-uneven number) is the host stitch. When the stitch enters a hole to return to the backface (down-even number), the element becomes the guest. The accuracy of one stitch determines the accuracy of all other adjoining stitches. If a hole that belongs to another stitch is used accidently, the smooth surfacing process of the primary fabric will be disturbed.

In addition, a change of material and size will substantially alter the impact of a stitch. It is important to have several different canvas swatches on hand and a variety of wool textures in order to be able to experiment with one stitch on different textures. There are certain stitches which simply look better on a coarser canvas, others in a finer one. The wool yarns which are the dominant canvas-work fibers used, vary in quality, weight, and finish.

Some weights are spun and plied for one size canvas; some might be too coarse for smaller size canvas, displacing the weave of the primary fabric. Some might have a ply that is too fine to adequately cover the primary fabric. Needles must be blunt so that at no time is either the warp or the weft of the primary fabric pierced.

The Family of Tent Stitches

Both the half-cross stitch and the diagonal basketweave look like the tent stitch on the frontface. The difference between these apparently identical stitches is recognizable at the backface and can also be quickly identified if all three stitches are used within one area. (*See* figures 98 and 107.)

The backface stitch of the tent or gros point is longer and more sloped than its frontface version. Although the stitch is angled left to right, the rows are worked right to left. It is, therefore, essential for the backstitch to move beyond the first stitch made so that it can resurface one hole beyond. A continuous forward and back, left to right (frontface), and right to left (backface) rhythm of wrist and hand is required. The advantage of this stitch is its ease of work and the very soft and slightly loose appearance of the stitch on the canvas due to the imperceptible padding by the backface stitch.

The slant of the half-cross stitch is from left to upper right and its frontface appearance is the same as that of the tent stitch. The difference lies at the back where the cross stitch can be recognized by a short straight vertical stitch. It requires a sharp downward tug. The resulting stitch is flat and tight and only requires half the amount of embroidery element. It is thus a cheaper stitch in terms of element consumed, but its wearability is not as good. (*See* figures 107a and b.)

The basketweave stitch combines the softer approach of the tent stitch and the firm tug of the half-cross stitch. It is named for its appearance at the backface where stitches are interlaced as in basket weaving. This stitch is worked in diagonal lines. After each slanted stitch at the frontface, the needle moves down at the backface in a long enough straight line to be able to resurface, ready for the next left to

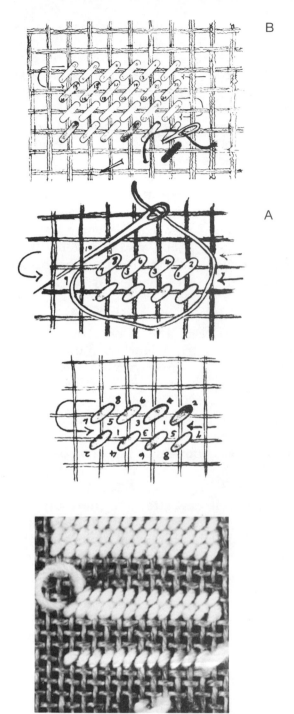

Figure 98. Tent stitch. Also known as tapestry stitch and continental stitch. Stitches always slant from left to right and rows are worked from right to left. Turn needlework upside-down at the end of every second row to assure uniform slanted stitches at the backface (version B). For frequent color changes, as in shading, use version A and reverse hand movement, stitch and row direction for greater ease. Drawings from *Victorian Fancywork*, (by Markrich and Kiewe), Henry Regnery Co., 1974, page 165.   Photo shows several rows of tent stitch with either stitch hand-movements or primary fabric reversed.

right slanted frontface stitch. With the next diagonal row, the stitches move upward from left to right fitting into the breaks between the stitches of the previous row, the back stitches appearing as staggered horizontal lines. The firm interlacing of the back stitches serves not only as reinforcement of the frontface slanted stitches but results in an extremely hard-wearing piece of canvas work. (*See* figures 108a-e.)

The overall-repeat satin stitch seen on the Mandarin Square is known as the brick stitch. Its frontface appearance is composed of carefully staggered, taut, straight, vertical stitches and obvious shadow breaks. The backface is horizontal lines of slanted stitches. (*See* figure 113.)

The vertical gobelin stitch appears structurally identical to the brick stitch at the first glance. The stitch is worked in upward moving, over-under-and-up diagonal lines. As the less rigidly tugged rows of stitches adjoin one another, one notices what seems to be a common stitch placement. The stitches of the former are, though, less taut and the shadow breaks less obvious. At the backface, the slanted stitches are short and barely cover the backface. (*See* figures 104-106.)

There is no better and more practical way to discover how to read and work canvas stitches, stitch units, and multiple stitch unit patterns than to take an 18-inch square of canvas and begin to experiment step by step. Instead of working single rows one should draw and define specific shapes on the canvas such as triangles, rectangles, circles and ovals. Do not work a design of equally sized squares; they do not permit the necessary practice of fitting a stitch into a certain shape. Carefully mark the lines on the canvas with India ink and a brush. A worked canvas may stretch and buckle out of shape and when completed must be blocked. Blocking requires dampness and felt-tip markers are not necessarily waterproof. It would be most unfortunate to have colored outlines bleed into the yarn.

Use one or several colors for any one stitch and shape. Just be sure that no two "identical" stitches are placed close to one another. Watch that stitch units requiring more than two holes are foreshortened or replaced by a few tent stitches to fit a certain stitch unit sequence within a specific area. Misapplication of such stitches can distort the design line. Try to balance stitches with obvious diagonal shadow break lines against those with vertical or horizontal patterning. (*See* figure 133.) Neutralize two equally strong textured stitches by inserting a tent stitch section. As work proceeds an authentic patchwork of color and stitch texture will develop. The satin stitch family will become familiar and the choice of a particular stitch for a particular area will cease to be a matter of concern.

THE FAMILY OF SATIN STITCHES

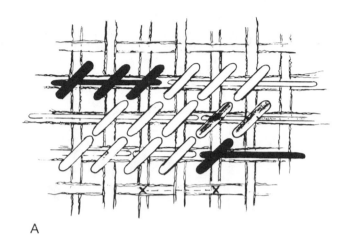

A

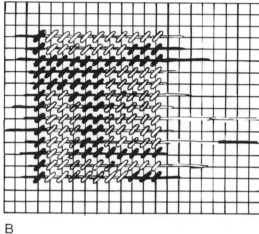

B

Figure 99. Trammé. Generally associated with lines of thread run across a commercial canvas to indicate a pattern, it is an important asset to raise (or pad), tent or half-cross stitches. Penelope or double-thread canvas is essential to lay the undercolor as a padding element either as shown in (B) or as marked on (A) with Xs on the lower line between one warp and weft intersection and another.

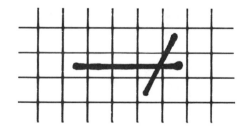

Figure 100. Trammé on single- thread (uni) canvas. On any single-thread canvas the working element is run horizontally from one canvas hole to another. That means that the stitch slanting across this laid line must use the line of stitch holes above and below the center line. The result is a larger stitch and one possibly unsuitable for the design. In both instances adjoining, top-layer stitches can be spaced close together or far apart. In the latter case the coloring of the horizontally laid element will be visible. During the 1920s and 1930s it became fashionable to embroider canvas designs in the trammé manner with a heavy yarn and to omit the second layer of stitching. It is an easy way to introduce young children to canvas work.

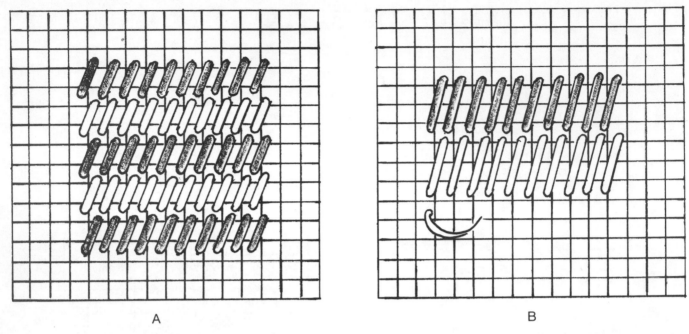

A   B

Figure 101. Gobelin stitch. A straight and long, slanted tent-stitch is generally known as a Gobelin stitch since its appearance is similar to the weft of a tapestry weave. The name does not, however, indicate the number of weft and warp elements that are crossed. Slant and height can vary but are never perfectly balanced. (A) Across one warp and over two weft elements. A stitch unit requires six holes. (B) Across one warp and over three weft elements. A stitch unit requires eight holes. Adjoining stitch lines butt against one another and the horizontal shadow-break lines are strong.

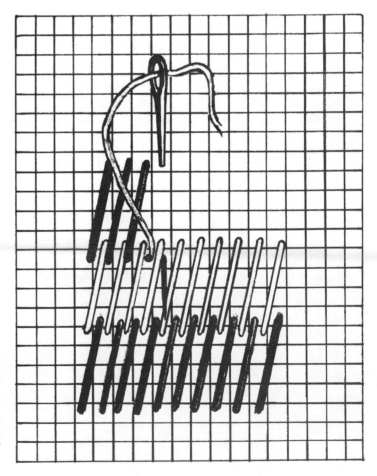

Figure 102. Encroaching Gobelin stitch. Excellent background stitch. If used for an overall, shaded design in a smaller size (instead of tent stitch), the outlines will be blurred and therefore softer. Stitches can be worked from right to left or left to right. To maintain an even backface stitch-sequence, alternating stitch-lines should be worked either clock- or counter-clockwise.

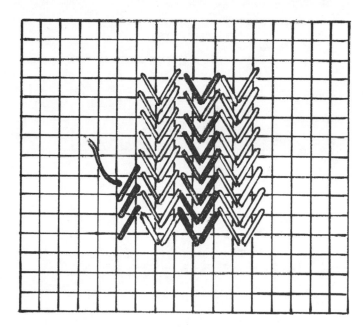

Figure 103. Knit or Kelim stitch. Two names which describe a pair of slanted stitch rows of stitches otherwise known as satin or Gobelin, and which move in opposite directions to form a chevron or herring-bone pattern. Rows can be worked horizontally or vertically. Interesting interlaced, geometric patterns can be designed by planning to use a pair or more of rows moving in both directions. In such a case, care must be taken to avoid uneven tension. The hand motions pulling the working element will differ in amount of tug. Solid or striped color effects. A stitch unit requires nine holes, across two warp and two weft elements.

Figures 104-106. Sloping Gobelin stitches. These three stitch variations are extensions of the stem stitch. Each one depends upon a forward and backward movement. Read number sequence carefully.

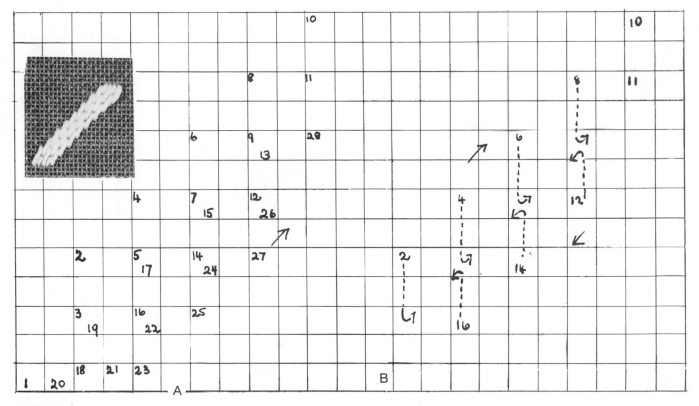

Figure 104. Upward diagonal slant. Backface (B) will show a series of straight perpendicular stitches. Practical as a filling stitch for shapes moving towards the right. Turn primary fabric and design upside-down to reverse direction (leaves, etc.).

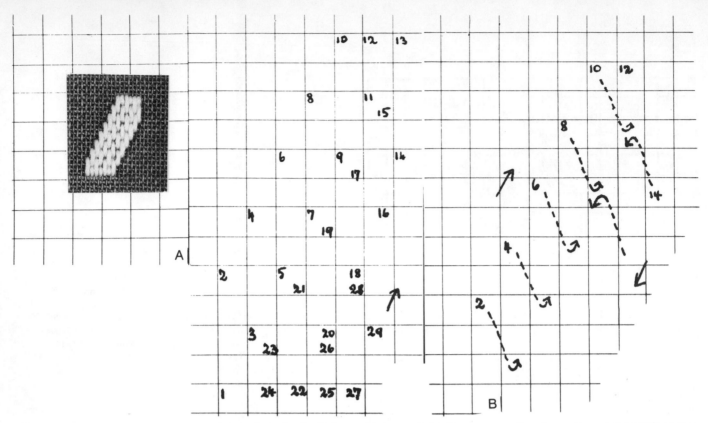

Figure 105. Moving upward in a series of vertical stitches which are linked to one another by a diagonal backface the overall appearance is similar to brick stitch. However, the shadow breaks are less pronounced and the overall appearance is softer as the working element moves upward instead of back and forth horizontally. Good background stitch. Interesting effects can be obtained. (B) is backface.

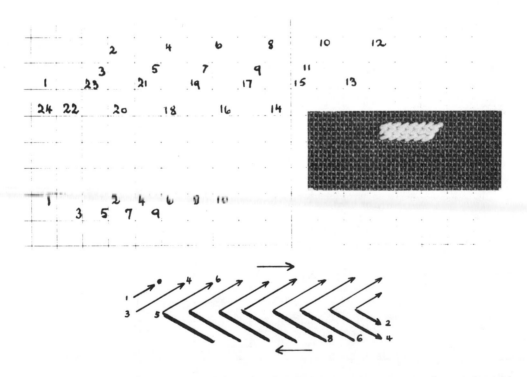

Figure 106. An interesting stem-stitch surface similar to the Soumak weave on rugs can be produced by working from left to right and right to left. If every stitch line is started at the left-hand side the texture will be smooth. A stem stitch on canvas would look best if the forward and back movement were carried along one weft element only.

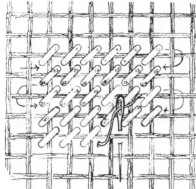

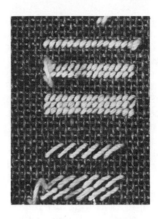

Figure 107A. Half-cross stitch, also sometimes known as continental stitch. Shading stitch. The downward tug required as the working element moves from one stitch to the next tightens the stitch. Less yarn consumption. Work both stitch rows and the stitch itself from left to right. Any row worked from right to left requires reversed hand movements to maintain short vertical-stitches at the backface. Drawings from *Victorian Fancywork,* page 164.

Figure 107B. 1st line is half-cross stitch. 2nd and 3rd lines or rows show a common needlework error—the use of the half-cross stitch for any long row of stitching from left to right and the tent stitch for the right-to-left line. The result is uneven stitching and undesirable. Last two lines show the large tent stitch called Slav stitch.

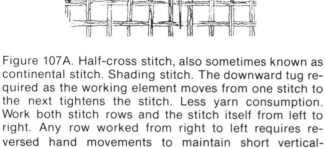

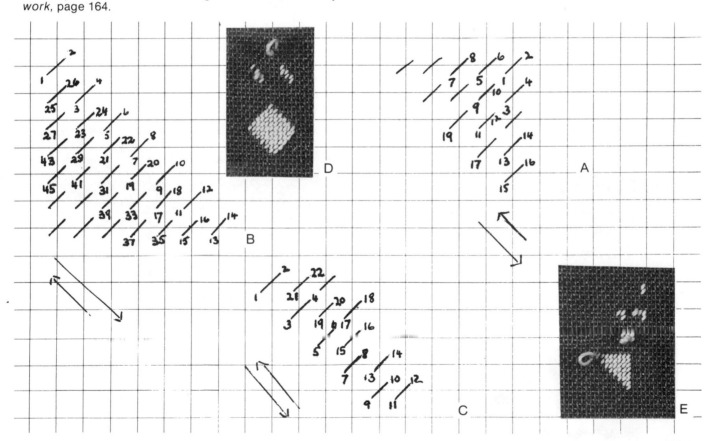

Figure 108. The diagonal basketweave stitch. This stitch owes its name to the interlaced pattern at the backface which prevents the slant stretch of tent-stitch embroidery. An excellent background stitch and well suited for non-shaded blocks of solid color on uni canvas. Its structure is based on a continuing series of diagonal, parallel, and encroaching tent-stitch lines. (A) The number sequence required when starting at the top right-hand corner, moving downward and extending the stitch line. (B) How to start at the top left-hand corner and move downward to complete one half of a background area. (C) Shows how to reach the top right-hand corner and thereby complete the upper half of section (B). (D) A single stitch, and a single line. Two lines and a sample shape. (E) Photo shows how the first stitches were placed for a sample shape.

Figures 109-118. Canvas satin stitch patterns based on diagonal lines. The names are varied and bear little relation either to the pattern design or authenticity of origin, nor do they indicate to a beginner the required number-sequence for stitch placement. Instead, these colorful definitions are the label someone at some point gave to a pretty stitch grouping and which in turn, during the 19th century, found its way into print as the mass production of stitch patterns got under way. The variations are as endless as personal inclinations can make them and as soon as any embroiderer understands their development there is little need to conform to the routine. Almost all of the standard repeats can be found on white linen-work of a period preceding that of Berlin-work. Their transition as easy, wool-work exercises is simply a demonstration of the satin stitch's ability to adapt itself to any fashion. Once any embroiderer understands how these patterns were developed by the simple expedient of adding a longer or shorter slanted stitch to form an already common pattern repeat—not only found in needlework but in other craft and art media—a personal interpretation and the discovery of another pattern adds to the fun needlework on canvas can provide. Like mosaics and jigsaw puzzles, every adjoining row must fit into the previous one and, sometimes, two parallel lines which do not interlock are joined by a third line which fills the gap of canvas and thereby creates another pattern. Mix and match is a suitable slogan for their variety. Remember, all have a definite and obvious texture and their shadow breaks must be compared to pencil-sharp line drawings on paper. Some are more pronounced in their design than others. They can run from upper left to lower right or lower right to upper left by repositioning the primary fabric. Some are good as background stitches, others better as detail accents. All are individualists and their usefulness as filling stitches is governed by their structure as much as the available area within the shape to be filled. The stitches shown were chosen to demonstrate how these patterns possibly evolved. Remember that supplementary foreshortened stitches must be added at the end or beginning of a line to conform to the required shape of the area being filled.

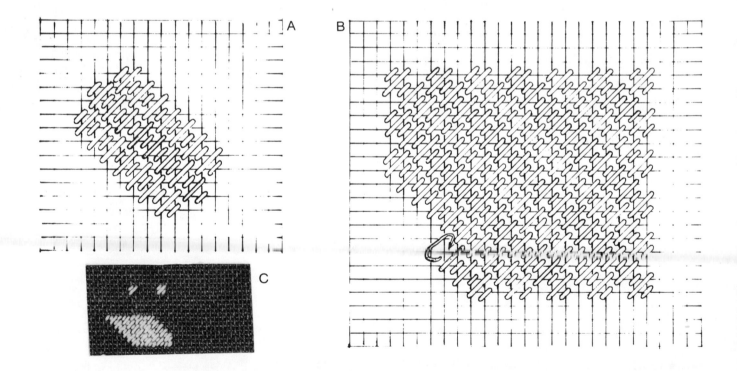

Figure 109. Diagonal Florentine stitch. The principle is the same as that of the diagonal basketweave stitch. Diagonal satin-stitch rows are worked in alternating up-and-down slanting movements. First stitch is identical to the tent. Across one warp and over one weft element. The second stitch begins beneath the first stitch and ends alongside it by moving across and over *two* warp and weft elements. Each succeeding stitch pair starts alongside the last stitch of the previous pair. Drawing (A)—from left to right. Drawing (B)—same stitch started at top right-hand corner. Note blanks at edges to allow for stitch adjustment.

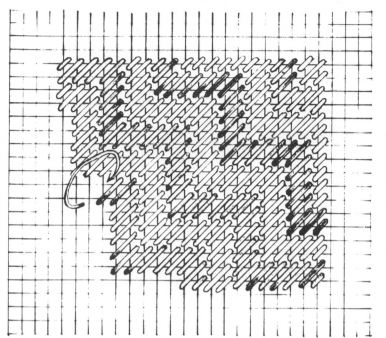

Figure 110. Byzantine stitch. Take any size slanted, satin stitch and work a set of stitches horizontally. Move downward and begin a perpendicular line of identical stitches below the last stitch of the horizontal line. When the last line is long enough, move across horizontally and repeat throughout. The last stitch of one line always serving as the first stitch of the next pattern shift. The result is a clearly defined zig-zag not only of stitching but of resulting shadow breaks. Any size slanted stitch with any length of horizontal or perpendicular stitch line grouped in this manner qualifies for a name which probably originated when someone saw the same pattern device on a Byzantine mosaic. Stitch unit—across two warp elements, over two weft elements, nine holes.

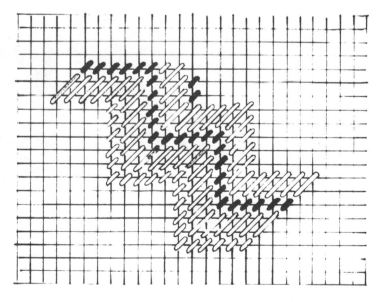

Figure 111. Jacquard stitch. Take a diagonal, slanted satin-stitch longer than the basic tent and work a row of Byzantine stitching. Instead of working back with a set of identical stitches, use longer or shorter slanted-stitches. Repeat these two rows throughout and the once balanced zig-zag lines will now appear in an alternating sequence. Joseph Marie Jacquard, born in 1752 in Lyon, France, perfected a loom conceived by B. Bouchon (1725) improved by M. Falcon (1728) and J. de Vaucanson (1745) for pattern weaving. The use of his name for a stitch pattern allows romantic assumptions but *not* the assumption that he designed the stitch! Stitch unit—hole requirement varies.

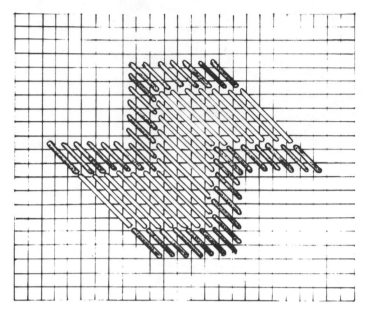

Figure 112. Jacquard stitch, size variation. Alternating start.

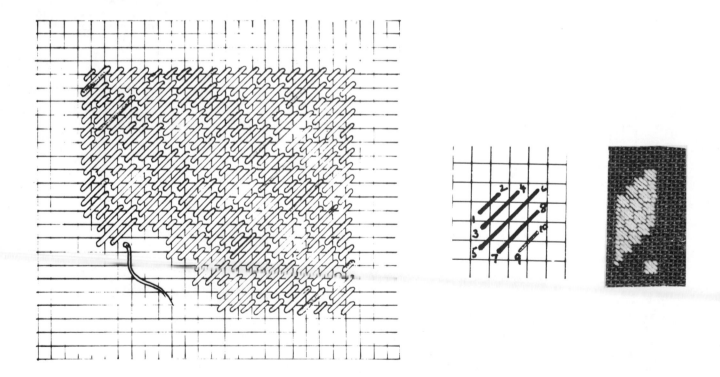

Figure 113. Diagonal-stitch square variations. Commonly known as the diagonal stitch, a line of successive squares composed of a set of carefully graduated slanted stitches is an easy and attractive pattern which lends itself well to solid or multiple-color interpretation. The lines can run in two directions and instead of just two colors, any number of color variations can be achieved by varying the distance between the colors instead of alternating two or more colors. Stitch unit—twenty holes. Note that the first three stitches start below one another (vertical shadow-break) and the last of these is the first of the three stitches of the second half, moving across horizontally.

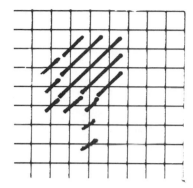

Figure 114. Moorish stitch. One diagonal line of squares and one line of tent stitches.

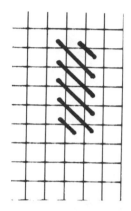
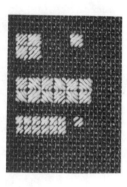

Figure 115 (A & B). Working with stitch squares. Interesting pattern and challenging color arrangements can be developed by working with squares of slanted stitches. Irrespective of their size, each square can be used to represent a square on a pattern chart, thereby increasing the size of the design and providing a technique similar to mosaic work. By varying the slant of the adjoining squares, an additional pattern becomes apparent and the difference in light reflection adds to the impact. The use of an overall geometric repeat of squares will also differ in appearance if the stitch rows are worked from side to side or up and down. Not only does the latter method seem to be faster but as the working element moves up or down after completing a unit, the first and last stitches of one square are not part of an adjoining structure and therefore a visibly more independent, precise square-shape appears. Recognition of such variables distinguishes the appearance of one piece of work from another. (A) Squares can be changed into oblongs by multiplying the number of central diagonal stitches.

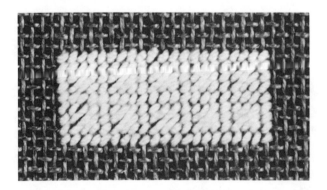

Figure 116. Scottish diagonal. At times there seem to be more Scottish stitches than villages in the Highlands. It is possible that due to the white-work cottage industries of the 19th century such pattern variations associated with fine, white satin-stitch embroideries became associated with Scottish work. This version consists of slanted-stitch squares framed by tent-stitch rows. Whether the squares should be worked first and the tent stitch later is a personal decision. Be sure to allow enough stitch holes for an overall repeat. Working a tent-stitch row first is probably easier for those who don't like to count more than once.

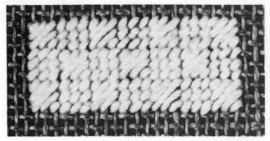

Figure 117. Checkers. Alternate one block of slanted satin stitches with one equal-size block of tent stitches.

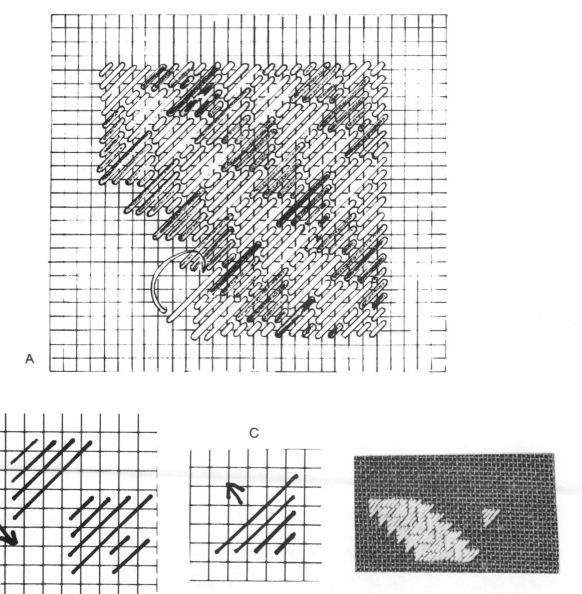

A

B

C

Figure 118 (A, B, & C). Milanese stitch. This is an enlarged version of the earlier diagonal Florentine. The number of slanted stitches has increased and the alternate rows fit into the spacing of the previous line. Remember that the longest slanted-stitch shares its holes with the shortest stitch of the opposing row. The shadow breaks will provide another zig-zag variation. Because the size of any triangular stitch unit can be varied no specific number of holes is given for the stitch unit.

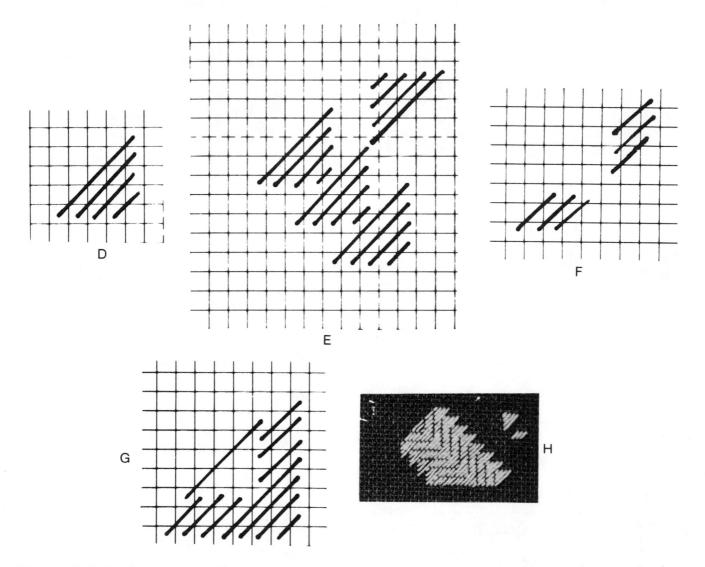

Figure 118 (D-H). Oriental stitch. The structural development of this stitch provides the clue of how to develop a personal stitch-pattern. (D) A diagonal row of a Milanese stitch sequence. (E) On the returning row, the longest slanted stitch of the new row butts against the longest stitch of the previous pattern-row. (F) The empty spaces are now filled with a third set of stitches. (G) Note the size of the triangle void. (H) Single color use with this stitch makes the third row indistinguishable.

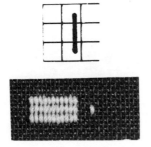

Figure 119. Satin stitch on canvas. Strong straight lines of color with sharp shadow breaks.

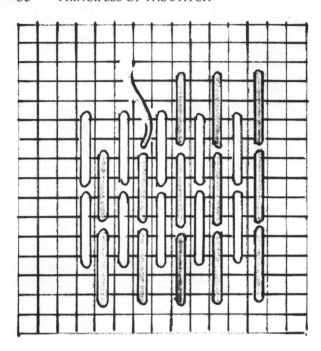

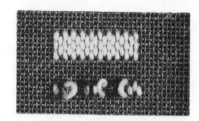

Figure 120. (Left) Brick stitch. Work one, skip one, and alternate the rows. Stitches can be lengthened or shortened to meet individual requirements. Turn primary fabric sideways to obtain a horizontal effect. Figure 121. (Above) Brick stitch on even-weave linen.

Figure 122. Alternating small and big is known as the Parisian stitch. Single unit—over one, over three, over one.

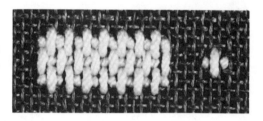

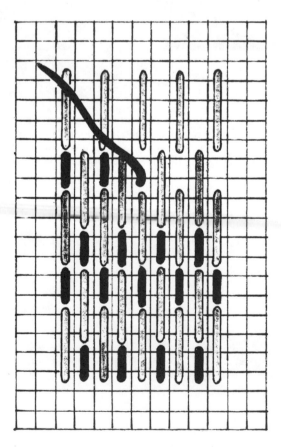

Figure 123. Alternating long and short stitches.

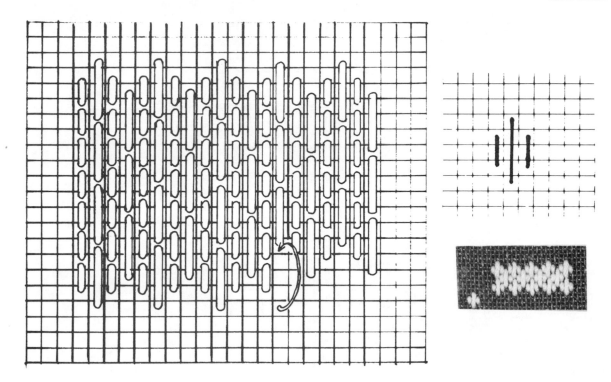

Figure 124. Hungarian stitch. Stitch unit—work from left to right and right to left. Excellent background stitch, shadow breaks develop a lozenge trellis work.

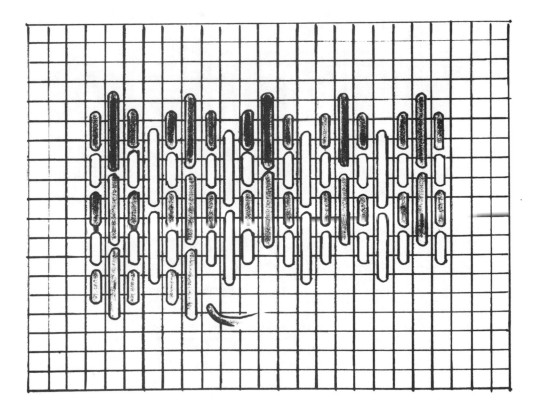

Figure 125. Hungarian stitch worked with two colors.

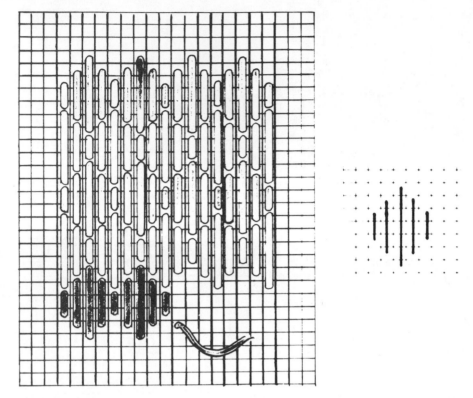

Figure 126. Instead of a space separating two units, the stitch unit has been enlarged and the first stitch of one unit is also the last stitch of its predecessor.

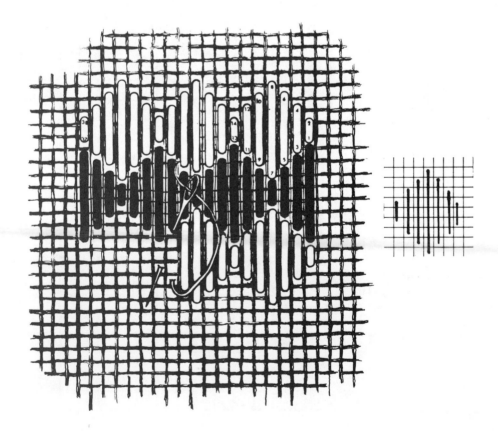

Figure 127. Seven stitches instead of five, and the effect is bolder.

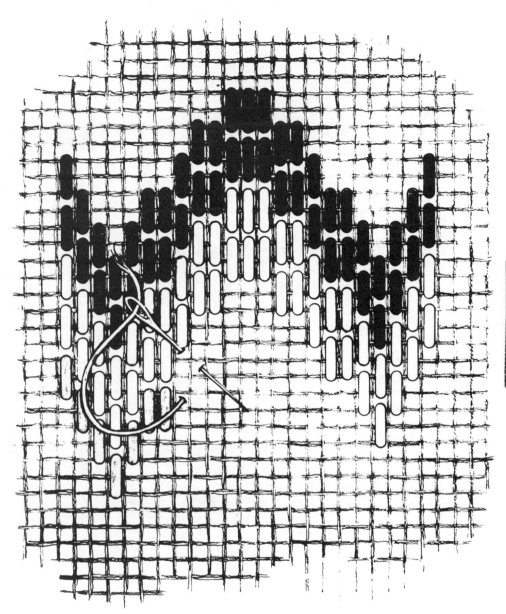
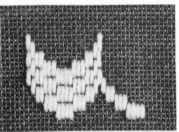

Figure 128. Florentine or Bargello horizontal line.
   (A) Crossing—each stitch crosses three weft elements of the
                primary fabric after the needle has surfaced.
                Therefore, three crossings require four holes.
        Stepping sequence—over three, back one. Complex patternings
                depend upon several stepping sequences.
                (Caution. Always study pattern charts carefully.)
        Grouping sequence—starting at top right-hand corner:
                four singles down; one, two, one, two, three up;
                two, one, two, two, singles down; three singles up.
                repeat this sequence throughout.
   (B) Crossing—four elements, five holes.
        Stepping sequence—over four, back two.
        Grouping—one, one, two, three, four, three, two, one.

Figures 129, 130, 131. Take any satin-stitch sequence, work it in horizontal or vertical lines, fill the center with a series of smaller horizontal or vertical straight-stitches, and another pattern has been developed. Colors can be bright or soft, blend or contrast—that must always be the embroiderer's prerogative. Long- and short-stitch rows are a simple but pleasing way to teach a small child to embroider and count.

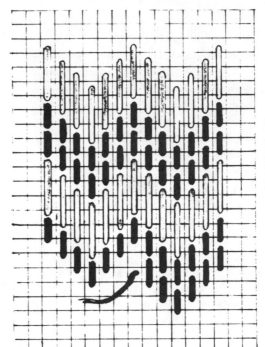

Fig. 129

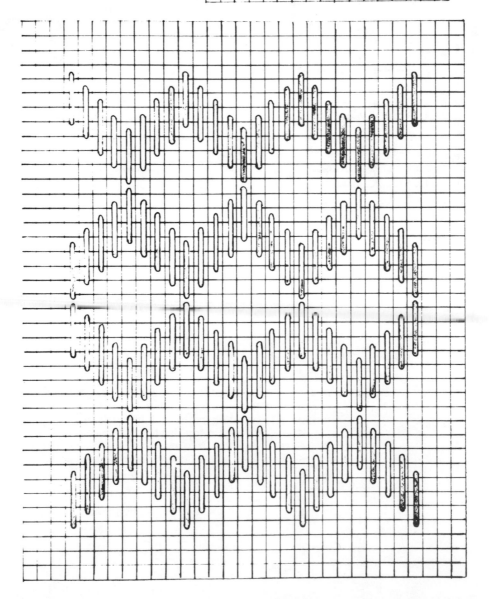

Fig. 130

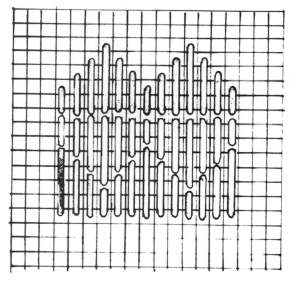

Fig. 131

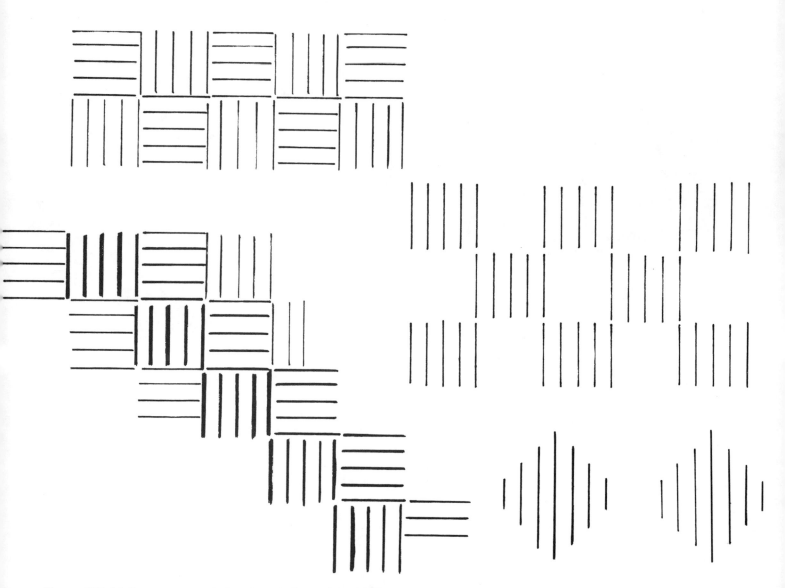

Figure 132. Make your own stitch unit variations of the basic satin-stitch by using a sheet of graph paper and drawing a set of lines. Pick favorite colors and a "new" stitch-pattern appears.

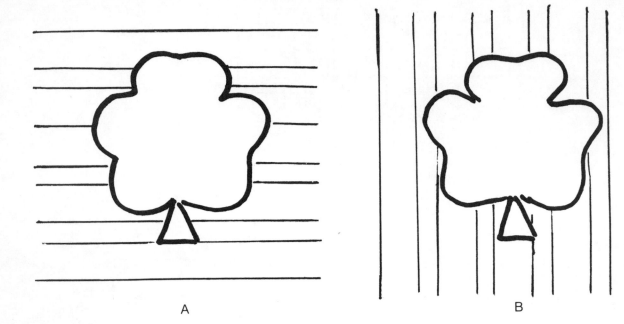

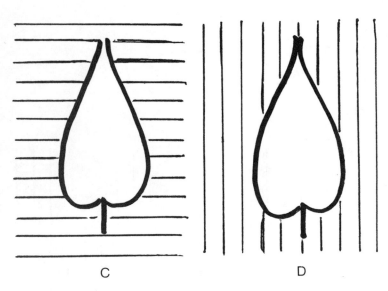

Figure 133. The influence of shadow break lines.
- (A) Broad shape on horizontal lines.
- (B) Broad shape on vertical background lines.
- (C) Narrow shape on horizontal background lines.
- (D) Narrow shape on vertical elongated background lines.

The Counted Satin Stitch

A different set of variations of the basic wrapping stitch is used as a geometric patterning device on a primary fabric with evident spacings between the interlaced warp and weft. The height, width, angle, or slant is controlled by the woven structure of the background material. To produce a stitch, the worker counts the number of warp or weft elements that must be crossed by the embroidery element as it passes from one hole to another. The crossings can be vertical, horizontal, or diagonal. The wrapping motion is either clockwise or counter-clockwise, depending on the need for forward or reverse motions. (*See* figure 127.)

All this demands is that the embroiderer's creativity be channeled differently. Individual stitches must be considered as square building blocks that must be staggered to achieve the illusion of a curve. It must be understood that a coarse primary fabric evenweave or with fewer holes to the inch will lend itself less well to creating the illusion of a curve. A primary fabric with a close weave that allows a larger number of holes, permits more stitches to move in the required direction. All motif outlines, even if traced with curves on the primary fabric, change into angular steppingstones as the stitches are placed side by side or are staggered.

Needlework styles such as *canvas work* that develop from this method of stitch use are simple. Instead of free-form stitch drawings, graph paper with squares representing holes is used to plan a design. The grid lines duplicate warp and weft elements; surfacing stitch holes are uneven numbers and entry holes are even. Individual stitch formations can be carefully blocked out ahead of time and then "read" and transcribed onto the primary fabric. Uncertainty of stitch appearance is minimized. New stitch units can be developed without previous art training by simply duplicating with a series of straight, parallel lines on graph paper any previously outlined shape or form. These new units should not be considered as new stitches. Rather, they are a new grouping of satin stitches. Used repetitively they form a design but no matter what the stitch unit or multiple stitch unit projects, the actual stitching is always the same, up-over-and-across-down-under-and back or across, and then up again

Figure 134 (A). Greek Island embroidery. Staggered satin stitch. Silk floss embroidery thread.

depending upon pattern stipulations.

Another style of needlework that depends on an open-weave primary fabric is counted-thread work, a simple and clear name for an easy needlework. Not all areas specializing in counted-thread work depend on the same motifs or use the same stitch patterns, but all of them share a common trait—the actual embroidery depends on the even weave of the primary fabric for its effect, and the fabric, however richly decorated with embroidery, is part of the overall design. The fabric acts either as a framework for embroidered sections or as an interruption to the flow of the embroidery element. Just as in the free-flowing embroidery style, the background color interacts with the design. In canvas work, stitches cover the primary fabric.

Pattern darning, cross-stitch variations, and satin blocks, all based on thread counting, are the dominant stitch structures found in peasant work. Pulled-thread work based on the tightening of the tug and pull of the satin stitch is another common form.

The geometric motifs in rural work are generally of religious or mystical significance and based on centuries of tradition. Over the years, the basic shapes have sometimes been modified by additional ornamentation or simplification. (*See* figures 134 and 135.) Central Europe and the Balkans, both linen producing areas with populations exposed for centuries to various cultural forces, have a rich, decorative history of counted-thread embroidery. Northern Europe, by contrast, tends to manifest a lighter and airier approach to white-on-white work. The satin stitch also dominated an embroidery style used extensively in the linen-growing areas of Europe. Popularly known as "white work," white opaque or translucent primary fabric was embroidered with such variations as linen on linen, linen on cotton, cotton on cotton, or fine linen and silk on gossamer white net. European white-work expertise had a long tradition as an essential part of ecclesiastical embroidery. Many convents and monasteries earned additional income for their orders by supplying embroidered linens for private chapels and secular patrons.

No nineteenth-century household linen

Figure 134 (B & C—top and middle) Details of Greek Island embroidery. (D—bottom) Backface of Greek Island embroidery.

Figure 135. Mandarin Square. China, third quarter of 19th century. Fretwork is stem stitch. Details are satin and tent stitch. (Author's collection.)

closet was considered complete without some hand-embroidered sheets and pillow cases. Christening robes and veils from Saxony (Germany) and narrow, multiple yard-long school samplers with white-work variations, and petticoat trimmings by the yard were *de rigueur* till World War I.

White work also reached every corner of the globe as nineteenth century trade increased and missionary schools were set up that included needlework in their curriculum. Their textbooks, based on the profusion of school-board specifications in London and Scotland, stressed the importance of good white work for the elementary school pupils attending non-private schools so that upon leaving, at the age of twelve or thirteen, they might increase their value as domestic servants by proficiency in repairing fine handwork. (*See* figure 136.)

The white work of Saxony developed in areas where an additional source of income was considered essential. The careful work of the women and girls, often trained at a nearby convent, guaranteed quality workmanship. The rates of payment were uniformly low, but the standards set required extraordinary expertise and time. The rates were lower, but the work was only valued as long as its standards were equal to that of the professional.

The embroidery, whether hand- or later machine-made, used the satin stitch to edge circular openings (cut work) by overcasting, to achieve a relief pattern or sculptured stitch density. The stitch's prominence intensified any white-on-white pattern, providing a contrast to the background texture. The basic raw materials were all standard primary fabrics and the embroidery and sewing elements readily available. There was no necessity to judge color from an artistic point of view and the emphasis was on technique and textural differences. There was no waste of thread, and, as in the case of innumerable cottage industries supplying domestic linens, farmers' wives could be employed cheaply.

By the latter part of the nineteenth century, Swiss embroidery machines and the lace industry of Nottingham produced exquisite white-on-white cut and lace embroideries by the yard, in all widths and all manner of pat-

Figure 136. Padded satin stitch. A portion of May Curd Sampler. (*See* figure 3.)

terning. It was such remarkably fine white work that a story is told of the time the owner of a famous factory was asked whether the piece of embroidery he was displaying was authentic (handmade). He answered with pride, "It is genuine machine-made." However minimal the labor rate for handmade work, it was impossible to compete with the machine, and the local industries declined and turned to other piecework. This was not true in the Far East, where trading houses had less investment in labor than in raw materials and shipping costs. In addition, certain convents depended on the excellence and artistic superiority of their work for the fame it brought them. These continued their needlecraft.

The commercial, mass production of white-on-white embroidery dealt the first blow to quality white work. As soon as cheap domestic labor ceased to be available to wash the white-on-white linens with the care they deserved, the demand further decreased. With improved mass transportation village girls left to work in an ever increasing number of local factories. Despite long hours they found that steady work, regular wages, and companionship were preferable to rural isolation, uncertain earnings, and the whims of the "mistress."

Today the satin stitch and other simple embroideries are still produced in the rural areas of underdeveloped countries, with minimal pay for the worker, while the white work of the past can be found only in antique shops and fairs.

8 Texture and Color

If the present day interest in embroidery is to be sustained, only an active return to the worker's prerogative to choose stitch and color (shade, hue, and tint) within the context of the design will prevent this ancient art form from changing into a sterile, programmed exercise.

The majority of beginner, intermediate, and even advanced embroiderers consider the personal stitch and color selection for their project a major obstacle. This phenomenon exists despite any needleworker's constant conscious and unconscious exposure to two neither unrelated nor insignificant factors. The first and the more obvious is the daily color assault on the eye via television, posters, magazines, color prints, and merchandising displays. The second and perhaps more subtle influence is the inevitable exposure to art reviews or criticisms in the daily press and magazines. Regardless of whether the critic lauds a passing art fashion or comments on a recent museum acquisition or gallery opening in a lengthy column, the illustration and the sentence which serves as a caption frequently increase the reader's awareness and sharpen his individual judgment. It is most curious that adults capable of making color and texture decisions when it comes to dress, furnishings, and lifestyles, feel restrained and inhibited when their personal preference must relate to such a simple craft medium as needlework. Before the marketing of the sealed embroidery kit as a practical, inexpensive labor-saving device for embroiderers became popular, sales personnel at needlework shops were enthusiastic participants in the selection of materials. They served as sympathetic sounding boards willing to share their experience with the customer. Their method of operation was very simple. The client stated whether the project was going to be self-designed, or based on a chart, a hot iron transfer, a stamped linen, a painted canvas, or whether it required a special order. Then a decision was made as to the best primary fabric, the type of stitches which might be used, and the cost, quality, and weight of the embroidery element. The client would next indicate how and where the object would be used and express color preferences; the shopkeeper would place on the sales counter the colors under consideration to give the customer a rough idea of their potential harmony or discord. A single skein of the basic color would be joined by color skeins of stronger or weaker intensity, softer or brighter hues, and their secondary warmer or cooler relatives.

Once the most favored deep, medium and light shades of a color had been selected, others were added. The quality of these efforts on the part of needlework shop owners and their personnel distinguished one store from another. It sustained those shops which survived the non-needlework years of the late twenties and thirties and forties. Theirs was a deliberate attempt to help translate a customer's fantasy into reality. Therefore, today, one of the first steps in banishing one's fears of selecting the yarns and other materials for a project is to find sympathetic sales personnel to help with the selection. Shops must be visited and their personnel evaluated. The problem of color selection within the realm of textiles does not only rest with the selection of favorite colors but with a willingness to explore, to experiment, and to understand the relationship between the materials. Without the correct fusion of materials the potential project, at this point only an imaginary concept, cannot become a visible reality. The old-time collaborators in color selection knew the potential advantages of every primary fabric and their most complimentary embroidery elements, and used this knowledge to assist those less experienced. Their goal (although they were the first to admit that a sale was desired) was to encourage and never to imply a lack of ability on the part of their client. They pushed, prodded, stimulated, and accelerated the customer's understanding while at the same time demonstrating how their own expertise was the result of personal needlework disasters and which in turn were utilized to serve as a preventive guide for others. They encouraged flexibility within the framework of the design and style. They took pride in their craft, and their commercial success was not only evaluated at the cash register but by the quality of the finished objects their clients produced.

Instead of nurturing inhibitions and being in awe, the embroiderer must display a willingness to experiment—ripping shading errors, adding another row of contrast stitching to a

receding color area—camouflaging early flaws until finally the most personally satisfying balance and harmony between primary fabric, color, and stitch texture has been achieved. Common sense, a keen eye, a sense of touch, and an unrestricted feeling for one's favorite colors—their harmonious extensions or contrasting possibilities—are what is important.

One of the tragedies of modern embroidery is that the average embroiderer has been unexposed to the previously discussed traditional methods of learning, and suffers from an acute and inhibiting syndrome known as "which stitch where." The energy which should be channeled into the imaginative use of color and texture as a means of projecting a personal interpretation of shape and form are often stifled by the fear that the stitch used might not provide the correct result. If however the embroiderer understands from the outset that stitches are flexible tools with many facets, and adjustable so that they can be grouped into individual segments, stitch combinations and stitch units—their use as a means to an end would be a less inhibiting force. No one can in good conscience claim to have been present when the first rules and laws relating to the use of stitches were proclaimed and the twentieth-century embroiderer must understand that stitches do not restrict imagination and that stitch rules are not binding.

Color and the Background

It is essential to approach any piece of needlework in a practical and fearless manner, although some trepidation remains even with the most skilled embroiderers. The following exercise should help the reader learn to evaluate not only a variety of shades but also a variety of stitch techniques—all which will help immeasurably in interpreting individual projects.

For this imaginary exercise, choose red as a background color, because red makes the interaction between the design, the stitches, and the primary fabric more obvious. It also requires a constant adjustment and shifting of color and stitches so that the strength of the primary fabric's color does not overwhelm the design (the exact reverse of white or natural background which makes no demands on the colored stitches of the embroidery, thus remaining unobtrusive).

White Work on Red

Let us assume that the piece is a stamped design of flowers, foliage, and stems, and is to be worked first with white throughout. White would show up clearly and every detail would be seen. If a needleworker simply used the stem stitch to follow all marked lines, the end result would simply show a white pattern against the red with little more impact than white ink on red paper. Let us assume though that the design has an important central flower surrounded by a series of coiling stems and assorted leaves. If a heavy, knotted linear stitch is used to outline the flower petals and in addition a heavier embroidery element is employed, that area of the design would suddenly demand more attention from the viewer since the heavier white outline against the inner red area would accentuate its color intensity. With the addition of a few simple thin lines of white stem stitch within each petal indicating light veining, the strength of the red background and the directional movement of each petal would increase. Despite an extended red background, the focus would remain on a red flower limited only by its thick white confines. Were the center of the main flower covered with a white filling stitch, the center would seem to recede and the petals to come forward, adding depth to the overall effect.

Obviously, the surrounding foliage of such a strong motif cannot and must not compete for attention. Rather, it should present a gentle and less obvious contrast. A first thought might be to outline each leaf with slender lines of single or double rows of stem stitch. Though not as strong as the flower, the introduction of a profusion of smaller, white-outlined red details would begin to dominate by dint of sheer quantity. But *filling* the leaves with rows of white stem stitch in a fairly uniform manner would provide a framework of white leaves for the red flower and decrease the impact of the actual red background. To simplify a decision, filling leaves with stitches identical to and of equal color impact and texture as those previously used for the flower's white center would detract from the flower's focal point.

Now let us assume that the flower at the center is to be white, not red. In this case, rich and intense white filling stitches such as Satin, Fishbone, Cretan (with its textured central line), clustered French knots, etc., could be used for the flower petals, and the leaves simply outlined with sparse white lines to permit red foliage.

A final comparison between the two variations would show that a red flower framed by white moves forward in spite of the red background, due to the surrounding framework of white leaves. On the other hand, the all-white flower appears to recede or move back, giving a feeling of space and depth. This is accentuated by the surrounding red-tinted foliage which moves forward and restates the overall color of the primary fabric.

Which interpretation is preferable depends entirely upon the needs and personal taste of the worker. It should be clearly understood that the basic balance of good needlework depends on the harmonious alternation and blend of a strong color or stitch in relation to a less obvious and weaker one. How to achieve this balance is a continuous and delightful challenge.

One-color exercises promote a feel for texture and an understanding for the difference in light reflection created by individual stitches. However, they can be exceedingly dull. For the present day embroiderer, the two-color impact of a one-color embroidery is of major importance in only two types of work. First when the stitch and design style, as in Assissi work, requires the complete covering of the background area by one stitch such as cross stitch. Such styles require the background material color to play an appropriate interacting part with the color of the embroidered stitches since the shapes of the motifs are left blank or void and are surrounded by background stitching. The second relates to needlework using a number of elements each of differing texture but of identical color. In the latter case the overall effect of the design is based on stitches most suited to the differing light reflections and textures of the fiber elements worked.

The majority of needlework styles are multicolored. Color is by far the most exciting, creative, and personal aspect of good embroidery. The texture of the stitch serves to reinforce or to weaken the impact of any shade or tint. After blending the red-colored primary fabric with richly colored embroidery elements, the original design, except for its shape, will bear little visual relationship to the earlier discussed two-color exercise. To discover which shades are best suited for the red of the primary fabric, only the old time-tested method of pulling out skeins and strands of yarn and putting them against the background material will give the embroiderer the closest approximate color effect. Instead of working with a fixed idea about color arrangement, the worker should constantly shift and rearrange shadings until, just before starting work, the embroiderer knows which of the skeins will be used for the more dominant and which for the less obvious areas.

Assume that the embroiderer chooses a soft, rich yellow to be the main color on a background primary fabric of red that veers toward the orange rather than deep blue. The yellow might belong to color ranges as different as buttercup yellows, orange yellows, creamy yellows, citron yellows, dull golds, mustards, or lime-green yellows. If skeins are unavailable and the yarn is sold by the strand, take several strands and bunch them together to get the proper color intensity. Within a short while even a novice will discover that color play is stimulating and challenging. Wrong color notes will soon become obvious. Good embroidery always requires more than one range of any one color used; so that using yellow as an example, the final selection should have one brighter range and one softer and—if the design permits—a third range too.

Once all the yellows have been selected, the additional colors required for the project will have to be chosen. By a steady process of putting shades against one another in good daylight, eliminating and reshuffling, the comparison between stronger and deeper contrasts versus softer and less obvious combinations can be seen. Deep brown or eggplant purple might appear strong enough to contrast well against the red background and serve to highlight the

previously chosen yellows when used in shading stitches. A medium shade of brown which looked interesting when held up against the light might fade into the red background and lose its value as a contrasting dark or light shade. Instead it might be used as a "drab," "snuff," or "sad" color unobtrusively worked within the shadings of stems and stalks to help link the more colorful flower areas.

A comparison of a variety of green color ranges for the foliage of the yellow blooms will probably indicate that shades of moss green and fresh apple green with a lime color for highlights will look better placed against the yellows and the red background than the colder blue-green and grey-green. In spite of the variety of yellows and greens selected for this imaginary design, the overall effect of just yellow and green on red would be monotonous without the addition of a few bright sharp tones of orange and red for smaller areas or shadings and perhaps the deep eggplant for the center of a flower.

Such an intense absorption in the selection of colors is time-consuming and emotionally demanding. Nor is it necessarily pleasing to a merchant. Nevertheless, any good and reliable store will welcome such interest on the part of the buyer since it displays a feeling for the medium used. Unfortunately even the most careful color selection will not guarantee a satisfying completed project, because the use of any stitch will vary the intensity and light reflection of the colored embroidery element in use and thereby alter its impact within the design. It is therefore necessary once colors have been chosen to use a stitch which by its texture and use will enhance rather than flaw its impact.

Flawed color selection, however, does not spell disaster. Often the addition of another color and stitch within the same area as in the case of an outline might suffice to add necessary depth or impact.

Only two things can really go wrong. The coloring and stitches may be too strong and overpowering for the overall design, or the shape may get lost in the overwhelming surrounding color of the primary fabric and adjoining segments of the pattern. Even then, all is not lost. If the overpowering area has been shaded with a long and short stitch, a few stitches of a softening color can be added. If linear shading has been used, individual rows can be gently pushed apart and another line of softer color run alongside. As for the lost leaf or flower, the addition of a strong textured outline with a more positive color might define the area. Such corrections work well if a careful and deliberate choice is made as to color and stitch. If the final result does not appear satisfactory, then a mild case of ripping with a sharp pair of cuticle scissors (which, thanks to their curve, slide easily under stitches) is in order.

Ripping or cutting out should never be equated with foolishness. After all, intent and fact are not always the same. If the "right" was not apparent before the "wrong," only elimination will clear the deck for the best end result.

There is no embroiderer who has not at some time or other discovered that several attempts with the same area of the motif have become exercises in futility. In such cases, it is best to forget about the whole thing for a while, move into another section and then return to the area after the surrounding motifs have been worked. Miraculously, the previously insurmountable obstacle can now be decisively and flawlessly completed. This is not due to magic but simply to the fact that the other areas are now visible and can reinforce or subdue the up-to-now missing link.

Working the Design

Once the selection of yarn has been made, the next point of indecision is generally where to begin. Resist the temptation to start on the most obvious and biggest details of the design. No matter how clearly envisioned nor how simple its requirements, once it has been worked it is there and requires every other shape to be cued to its color and texture. Instead of the balanced whole, the center might develop into a competitive area. In reverse a weak central area due to unfamiliarity and inhibition might later appear within the design as a core of dullness or an empty well as the more vivid and brighter surrounding areas, the result of increasing confidence with stitch use and color, attract greater attention.

It is therefore more practical to proceed slowly and become more acquainted with the design itself. After starting to work in a corner area with simple nondemanding stem stitch stalks or stems, the next step could be deciding how to work the adjoining leaves. There are many alternatives. All leaves could be filled with long and short stitch shading, or some of them could be outlined with a double row of stem stitch or one heavy stitch and the outer or inner curve highlighted by a thinner line of linear stitching in a darker or brighter color. Other alternatives include filling the leaf with linear shading or with a solid color stitch like satin, working the lower foliage in a deeper tone, the middle leaves in a medium range and the top leaves in a lighter, brighter shade.

As the first leaves are worked, the eye begins to familiarize itself with the adjoining shapes and one can conceive more clearly the development of the entire piece. Leaves surrounding a large central flower are small, busy details which might easily detract from a major decorative interpretation of the bloom. The use of unobtrusive color, blending with long and short stitch—possibly with shadings of green—will eventually provide an effective background for any flower of multicolored and multitextured appearance.

The shape of the central imaginary flower is irrelevant at this point. Its petals can be oval, pointed, or rounded at base or top. Their shaping can be circular, angular, or a series of slanted squares. It is any embroiderer's prerogative to decide whether to fill any petal with solid stitch patternings. Another decision is required when a choice is made whether to cover an outline with a line of bold color texture.

If the petals adjoin one another, the embroiderer has several alternatives. Each petal can be outlined by the use of bold linear stitches and patterned or shaded in the central area. Adjoining petals can be separated from one another by leaving a void, (a narrow band of unworked background) with the primary fabric color serving as a dividing line. Each petal can be filled with filling stitches which stop at each outer edge and butt against one another. The petals are then separated by the shadow break of contiguous stitches, or the embroiderer can decide to ignore all individual petal markings and treat the entire floral area as a stylized whole. Complex stitch combinations requiring moderate to larger areas for their visual effectiveness lend themselves well to such a stylized interpretation of a design. Without adequate space, complex stitch patterns—the result of multiple stitch application—cannot adequately display a good balance of texture, color, and interaction with the visible background. Unless simple basic stitches are used in the surrounding areas of the motif (leaves, outlines, stems, etc.), the effectiveness of intricate filling stitches is lost. Simple stitching is the essential harmonizing link between one section of the design and another. The elaborate and the obvious or strong must always be balanced against the plain, the softer, or the weaker.

The Visible Background Color

The background primary fabric is a very important element in any embroidery and should not be neglected in the course of planning a project. Its influence is increased or diminished by the strength and color of the surface stitching and regulated by the distance between stitch units and lines. It is necessary to keep in mind at all times this delicate relationship. (*See* figure 137.)

Seeding

There are several techniques that can be used to give an area the impression of open rather than opaque patterning. The simplest of these is seeding. For especially large, bold areas several different stitches can be combined to produce stitch units with distinctive patterning, which are then scattered haphazardly over the working area.

Diapering

Another useful patterning device is diapering— the covering of any area with a precise arrangement of diamond or other repeated shapes. In needlework, as in any other art medium, there is no rule as to decorative impact of these geometric shapes. They can be closely-spaced, alternating blocks of stitches divided by voided lines of the visible primary fabric; they can be groups of stitches shifted to present a diamond-shaped image and placed in an alternating sequence. (*See* figures 130-132.) As in every other area of embroidery, the number of possibilities is limited only by the quality and enterprise of the individual worker's imagination as he combines several stitches to form a single pattern unit and then repeats it in diagonal, horizontal,

Figure 137. Color and design. One basic shape and four simple interpretations. (A) Faint line or narrow stitch, faint color. (B) Medium thickness, stronger color. (C) Heavy outline stitch and stronger color. (D) Filling an area without an additional outline.

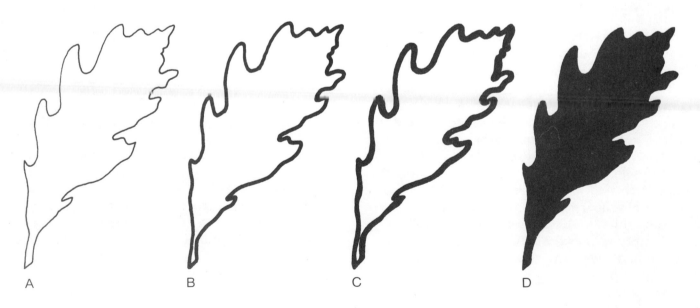

A   B   C   D

or vertical lines of equal or differing distance. Such a process is a creative use of stitching by any embroiderer. Essential to remember is that this patterning device adds perspective. The feeling of peering down or "openness" of the pattern lends itself well to any area where more than just a simple seeding on the primary fabric is called for.

The more intricate and time-demanding the patterning, the more it requires an adequate working area. It is foolish to try to squeeze groupings of minute Holbein stitching within a multi-faceted outline. The most effective diapering effects are achieved by simply crossing diagonally-laid embroidery elements and using the couching stitches as additional patterning devices. If diapering is not as simple as the alternating squares of a chess board, then it is only a matter of readjustment to lay embroidery elements horizontally and vertically and couch them diagonally with one small straight stitch, or other decorative stitches, in order to gain the desired box-like effect.

How the laid threads are spaced depends on the required size of the shape. The embroidery elements might be single, double, or treble units. Colors might be solid, shaded, or in the case of the triple unit, a light or dark shade framed by contrast in tone or color. The color of the primary fabric visible in the open spaces adds to the perspective and depth. (*See* figure 41.)

After the diagonal lines have been laid and crossed, the meeting points are tied down with either a straight vertical or horizontal stitch, or clusters of stitching to add pattern variety. The embroiderer can decide whether to leave all inner areas unworked in order that the background color may be clearly seen or begin filling in alternate or all spaces with other stitches.

The color impact of patternings which are more "busy" due to their use of several stitch layers must be approached with more than the usual care. If the background color of the primary fabric is left unworked, all patterning must be geared to enrich its color value. In the case of the red background, there would be little purpose in working a detailed diapering in a blend of reds since this would be lost by the overwhelming intensity of the background col-

or. Instead, a deeper or lighter color should be used which, together with the background color, would clearly define the basic patterning. This in turn could be enriched by the addition of other shades for the purpose of couching down embroidery elements and filling in central areas.

The use of an assortment of contrasting and competitive shades, however, can detract from the effectiveness of the patterning. This leads to a simple and practical rule of thumb. If the stitching is elaborate and intricate in appearance, avoid the use of an unlimited number of colors and concentrate instead on a blend of shades which will show up well against the primary fabric. For instance, if a white embroidery element is laid across the red primary fabric and a rude orange is used to tie it down, both red and white would have to give way to the ostentatiousness of that one orange stitch; by contrast, suitable shades of soft orange yellows on a coral red tied down with white would please.

Another example is seventeenth-century England, as the great period of crewel wool embroidery known as Jacobean work shifted from multicolored and gracefully flowing work to the heavy, cumbersome, one or two color-toned, elaborately patterned and textured textiles. At the beginning of the century, the first arrival of large quantities of Far Eastern textiles in silk and cotton had inspired a new fashion and revolutionized embroidery design. There was a happy and spontaneous fusion of Far Eastern and Western style and the great skills of the Elizabethan-period embroiderer made an easy transition from familiar shapes to the new. Over the years as projects became larger (bed hangings and coverlets) the once elaborately detailed designs were simplified and individual motifs enlarged. Such a coarsening of design required speedier stitch methods for filling large areas. By the end of this style period, embroideries were not judged by the quality of their design and appropriate workmanship, but rather by the imaginative combinations of simple stitch groups transformed into multilayered and multipatterned stitch details. Virtuosity and impact had replaced balance and harmony. It is interesting to note here that when a fashionable needlework style was based on stitch intricacy the quality of design usually was marked by a decline. The sixteenth century English blackwork embroidery fashion of fine, black silk on gossamer, white linen was one such period. Embroiderers—both professional and amateur—achieved a wide range of the most subtle tone variations of black on white by developing their own system of pattern repeats. Each one modified the interaction between the black stitch-pattern and the white background. The degree by which the latter intruded onto the pattern or was covered by stitching was based on the most knowledgeable and imaginative use of simple straight-stitching based on the running stitch. By the use of double running or double darning—a technique familiar to anyone—decoratively detailed and elaborate geometric shapes evolved. These patternings were seldom identical on both sides of the fabric but the double darning system did allow for reversibility. Although these stitch patterns show incredible and innumerable variations and tonal degrees, as seen by the billowing sleeves and coifs of the period on period portraits, the repetitive motifs used in blackwork—although charming—can hardly be classified as original examples of great embroidery design.

There is another group of stitches that by their quality or placement permit the intrusion of the background to increase the three dimensional value of embroidery. These are the stitches based on looping and knotting. They can be divided into two categories. The first, worked into the fabric, are attached knots and loops. To the second group belong those based on ancient off-loom looping and knotting techniques. These stitches were popular during the Renaissance as a means of producing fine linen lace with a needle instead of bobbins and were known as needlepoint. Their use as a needlework stitch must therefore be considered as an additional surfacing device which rests on the

Figure 138. Butterflies. Almost every possible variation of closed against open work, texture against smoothness, dark against light, and smooth against rough can be found in the butterflies. (*See* colorplate 6 for complete view of this work.)

Courtesy of Dr. Elizabeth Johnston

Courtesy of Dr. Elizabeth Johnston

Figure 139. Flowers. Bullion-knot petals clustered for texture and color variation. Softly shaded. Leaves in long and short stitch. Solid-color leaves in block stitches would eliminate the effect of the bullion petals. (This is another detail from colorplate 6.)

background of the primary fabric and is only attached to it at the outer edges. By controlling the tension of the embroidery element, the needleworker can adjust the spacing of individual knots or loops of the more opaque versions and thereby control the amount of visible background coloring.

A popular embroidery device during the Elizabethan period, these needlepoint stitches were the practical means of using gold embroidery elements on the rich silks. With the addition of bright silk embroidery elements under the gold, professional embroiderers filled flowers and shapes with brilliant impact. The use of needlepoint lace stitches as a means of lightness and openwork is all too often neglected by today's embroiderer despite the fact that the exponents of contemporary stitchery have long used these techniques to achieve soft sculptured effects. (*See* figure 138.)

Outlining

If these three groups of open work—the scattering of stitches by haphazard or carefully programmed means, the laying and couching of embroidery elements, and the use of textured lace stitches—are to be effective, then the shape they fill must be distinct, the outline not overpowered by the intricacy of the filling. (*See* figure 139.) The outline itself must be sharp and clear; the use of heavily textured and wide linear stitches would detract from the carefully built up pattern. A single row of stem stitch worked with fine thread would be a spineless divider, while a row worked in a heavy element would give the impression that the worker had become bored and was trying to finish hurriedly. The heavy chain, worked with small stitches in a good clear and sharp color, slightly more raised than the chain stitch, its loops re-

Figure 140. Late 16th-early 17th century. Embroidered Elizabethan bookbinding with couched gold thread outlines. Tent stitch on canvas. Gold- and silver-covered silk threads were knows as Cyprus, Damascus, or Venice gold. A guild known as the Gold and Silver Wyre Drawers, eventually granted a Royal Charter by James I, handled the domestic manufacture.

sembling a close plait rather than the obvious detail of the usual chain stitch, is by far the easiest and most suitable linear stitch. Seventeenth-century pieces show the use of fine braid-stitches or substitute a length of braid and couched gold elements to outline and define the individual petals and shapes of elaborately worked areas. The braid clearly defines the shape without detracting from the skilled patterning of the inner area. (*See* figure 140.)

The outline stitches required to give a crisp edge to any shape should be worked last. The outline is a finish; its color must depend upon the effect of the central area, just as its strength or thickness must accentuate and define the shape. If an outline is worked first, it will, because of its obvious visibility, immediately influence the embroiderer's choice of color for the inner area of the motif section to be worked. Since the entire area must play its part within the overall balance of the finished piece, it is better to work within the area first, and then to enclose it either by stitching in a contrasting color or with a lighter or deeper blend of one of the shades used for the central area. Also, it is easier to lay embroidery elements first or fill an area with an overall repeat and then to work the outline across both fabric and stitch fragments, thereby eliminating any rough, untidy, outer edges.

Solid Color Block Fillings

The large petaled flower, if surrounded by foliage of shaded long and short stitch, can be filled with a strong blend of coloring in the same stitch, of variations of linear stitching, or in any manner of openwork patterning, as long as each motif (petals, etc.) shape is defined by a clear outline to prevent the outer area of the primary fabric from dominating by merging with the open spacing of the flower shape (unless of course the embroiderer chooses such an effect). There are, however, additional stitches which owe their effect to constant repetition. Some of the best known of these are the fishbone, the Cretan, and the Romanian stitch which are textured rather than flat stitches.

The importance of these stitches lies in their usefulness as solid color blocks, each consecutive stitch adding to the clearly visible textured line or pattern within the central or outer area of its structure. Their use within large areas (petals, leaves, etc.) must be approached with care. The embroiderer must carefully evaluate the shape rather than the stitch, and decide the best way in which this large area can be divided so as to retain its original feeling. The focus must always remain on the central, solid-color stitch. The surrounding framework must recede both in texture and shading. Since embroidery is not a matter of copying natural shapes in a natural manner, it is once again the embroiderer's prerogative to try anything once. (*See* colorplate 8 .)

Shading

Shading within any filling stitch other than the long and short stitch, with its flexible streaks of dovetailed coloring, is never effected in the natural manner. But the willing and patient needleworker can add color variations not only to the filling stitches related to crewel and other embroidery styles, but also to the blocks of color associated with stitch units in canvas work. The method is very simple. Since all these stitches must conform to a certain sequence which cannot be interrupted, the use of one color for one stitch and the use of another color for the next stitch is marked. A "break" in the color line thus becomes obvious—an embroidery factor which is advantageous if the interruption of a color is required.

Let us assume that the colors of a worker using a good range and a suitably fine embroidery element are a, b, and c (this technique will only work if more than one embroidery element is used within the needle and the colors selected blend rather than contrast with one another). The worker threads five needles, one with two strands a, one with a & b, one with two of b, one with b & c, and one with two of c. The needleworker will find that instead of three different shades he now has five very subtle shade variations. By starting with needle

Figure 141. One of a pair of panels. China 18th century, Ch'ing Dynasty. A pair of cranes stand on a cliff separated by a large eroded rock covered with fungus and a peach tree. All are symbols of longevity. Two bats are symbols of happiness. Peony is the flower of riches and honor. K'o-ssu (slit-tapestry weave). Silk warp. Weft is silk and gilded paper wrapped around silk core. TM 51.60B.

a, and then changing over to each successive color blend, despite the fact that each stitch is an independent unit which must be completed before the next one is begun, the shift from one tone to the next is softened by the use of the double thread blend. (*See* figure 141 and colorplate 11.)

Where the transition from one color to another begins is entirely up to the embroiderer. The actual shape of a stitch will, of course, be more obvious during the transition from one tone to another, but some stitches

seem to thrive on this technique. These textured stitches—thanks to looping, crossing, or knotting—seem to slide or cup into one another so that the beginning and end of one stitch is intertwined with the next stitch. When a needle blend of color change is used for these stitches, the colors begin to fuse into one another. This is especially true of the many crossed canvasstitches where, instead of completing a stitch, the new color used for the last movement of one stitch crossing over the previous shade automatically becomes the beginning movement

Courtesy of The Textile Museum

of the next stitch. The shading is thereby layered in a most imperceptible manner.

The effectiveness of such shading depends upon the needleworker's imaginative use of the line direction which each stitch structure demands. When the needle blend of shading is adapted to the row direction of the stitching, and each adjoining line of color is either shorter or longer than the previous one, the embroiderer can produce carefully modulated shading of bright or soft coloring within an area generally considered suitable only for a solid color impact.

Shading on Canvas

Due to their structure, canvas stitches do not permit the easy curving of a line as in linear stitching, or in the placement of a series of individual stitches. Instead each stitch has its definite place. Other adjoining stitches may neither impinge upon the first stitch nor vary their distance from it. It is because of this inherent rigidity that shading in canvas embroidery presents difficulties. In canvas work, the agonies of shading are so pronounced, they frequently serve as a deterrent to finer work. (*See* colorplate 12.)

On canvas, it is the minimal stitch which enables a worker to achieve an illusion of curves. Therefore, canvas shading requires the tent stitch. This stitch requires two holes, crosses only one warp and weft intersection, and, by resting diagonally on the surface of the canvas between two identical stitches above and below it, thus acquires the manipulative qualities of a mosaic fragment.

Freeform stitches can always be adjusted in size. They can be foreshortened, slanted, literally squeezed into a space to supplement or widen; or, together with another stitch, they can be made to conform to the required design shape regardless of the primary fabric structure. In canvas work, however, the stitch is not just a decorative feature resting on another primary surface. By its interlocking action of sharing holes, the stitch produces its own background. Therefore it is color and not stitch that indicates the shape and form of a design. It is thus important that the embroiderer achieve the illusion of blended color and curves by the

careful placement of colored tent stitches.

Shading depends upon the flow of one color into another. Few objects depend solely upon straight lines of color for their form. It is therefore not the straight line which causes major concern in canvas shading but the curved line, which is controlled by stitch placement. If the tent stitch with its left to right slant is worked in a diagonal colored line starting at the left corner and moving upward to the right, the line will be smooth. If the same stitch has to produce a colored diagonal line which runs from lower right to upper left, unless the embroiderer does the unforgiveable and switches the slant of the stitch, a straight smooth line becomes an impossibility. Instead every succeeding colored, slanted stitch must be carefully placed either one step above and across, or one step across and below the previous stitch. Only by this system of staggered stitching will a diagonal be possible, opposite in direction from the slant of the stitch. Curving will depend upon staggering a series of stitches in a color contrasting to that of the background stitching and the sequence will give the illusion of a curve but it is actually based on a series of diagonal stitches placed either above or below one another, and then moved either above or below and across towards the left or to the right, depending upon the direction required by the stitch.

The most simple rule of thumb for canvas shading is to avoid any color lines which meet at an angle unless your design plan calls for geometric lines. If in doubt, work one color stitch less rather than more. Think of your stitch lines in terms of open-spaced staggered curves which must be filled by other curves of open-spaced staggered lines of stitching. Whether the curves are to shape fruit, clothing details, animals, or flowers and foliage, every stitch must be placed between two other stitches.

The actual shading depends upon the embroiderer's ability to shape with a grouping of slanted stitches. Staggered stitches obviously will produce gaps. These gaps have to be filled by background stitching before the project can be considered complete. If the outline simply indicates shape, the other colors must of course be used to fill the open inner space. It is here that the ability to blend yarn within the needle becomes a canvas embroiderer's greatest asset. Blank spacings can be filled by one or two stitches of a transitional blend consisting of shade a and shade b. By the subtle change of color each shape can be intensified or blurred and only by the use of needle-blended embroidery elements will you escape the hazards of blunt shaping and shading. The use of two needle-blended embroidery elements makes the difference between the subtle and the heavy hand. A single stitch of the slightest color variation at the base or top or side of any block of stitches will immediately alter the shaping of the surrounding area. (*See* colorplate 13.)

Outlining Solid Color Areas

Irrespective of whether the inner area of a shape is filled by freeform stitches, or, in canvas work, by a multiple stitch unit patterning, or by the simple tent stitch, the matter of outline cannot be ignored. There are basically three alternatives: using another stitch as an outline, leaving space between areas so that the primary fabric or a shadow break serves as an outline, or eliminating the outline and depending on skillful use of background color to define the shape.

The use of a secondary stitch would result in a marked contrast in tent stitch embroidery and might even detract from the quality of the filling stitch in other work. Outlining areas by means of a carefully-couched gold embroidery element was a popular and common custom in the Renaissance, as was the use of cord and braid. Basically, the choice of outline depends upon the design's need. If it is simple, the use of the slender stem stitch in an unobtrusive color (receding rather than forward moving) will do well. If a filled area lacks strength, the outline stitch and its color can be used as a balance.

An alternative to an outline is to permit the primary fabric in freeform embroidery, or the background color in canvas work, to act as a buffer between each section. In this case, the design and embroidery colors should be selected with this factor in mind.

The third and last option eliminates the use of outlines and focuses entirely upon the skillful use of stitch and color to emphasize the shape and form of an area. (*See* colorplate 12.)

Color as a divider between one area and another requires little more than the careful use of either a lighter or darker shade of color against an adjoining one. If, for example, two free-form petals are worked with a canvas stitch in a solid blend of color and an outline is omitted, the use of identical colors at the adjoining edges will interfere with the individuality of each shape. If, however, by the use of linear shading in free form stitching or the blending of embroidery yarns within the needle, the base or tip of each petal has been highlighted rather than the adjoining edges, then the petals will retain their separate identity. In the case of tent stitch shading, separation by color is entirely dependent upon the contrast in color and shade intensity between two stitches or two stitch lines. The most common error of any novice who works two identical joining petals with the same color is the sudden discovery that the clearly marked inked line on the canvas has been obliterated by the stitching, and that instead of two petals there is now one rather large and unwieldy shape.

The patterning of large stylized shapes—whether with geometric repeats (diapering) in free form stitching or with canvas stitch units which require more than just two holes (as the tent stitch) for their correct sequence—requires special attention. Accidental distortion of a shape can occur if smaller, supplementary stitches are used to fill in those gaps of the primary fabric which are not big enough to permit the proper sequence to be placed within a designated area. Although these additional stitches or partial stitch units are essential to prevent blank spots, the contrast between the supplementary stitching and fundamental patterning is strong enough to give the impression that the actual shape is related to the area completed by the main group of stitches. The additional filling stitches tend to blur the color of the main stitch and therefore can distort the outline. To prevent this, unless a blur is preferred, the outlines should be worked first so that the stitch grouping can be suitably adjusted within the area and the shape is properly defined. This is of special importance when textured stitch units worked on canvas are used to fill a certain area. An outline of tent stitch before filling will prevent a stitch unit usurping a hole meant for the final definition of the shape.

Conclusion

Good needlework requires that an embroiderer, regardless of personal preference as to style, be involved with and absorbed by the object as it grows and develops. The act of stitching—the actual physical action required to move a needle in and out of the fabric—is such a natural motion once it is mastered that all creative energy can be focused on the decisions relating to color and texture. Long apprenticeship in any craft taught this discipline together with another of equal importance: a personal sense of accomplishment.

When the old Guild system was still powerful enough to exert its strength and to control the quality of any object sold by one of its members, the workshop owners could not have functioned without a pool of cheap labor based on long apprenticeship. Women before the development of the Industrial Revolution with its mass manufacture of domestic textiles could not have supervised the production of handspun, handwoven, and handsewn materials for their household's clothing and furnishings without a long-term training period from early childhood in schoolrooms and home environ-

ment. Whether professional or amateur, both groups were taught that the ultimate reward for their efforts and skill was their personal sense of accomplishment for an object well made and worthy of recognition.

The technical skills were taught with a discipline and rigidity incomprehensible to today's rediscoverers of the once familiar ancient skills. Once learned they provided artisans with an inherent craftsmanship second to none. These were forever lost as expediency became a way of life.

Stitching, until the nineteenth century, was never a self-conscious exercise learned as participation or involvement in a current fashionable trend, but rather the result of hand movements used as unconsciously as raising a spoon to one's lips.

Thought and attention focused on the best interpretation of a design, colors, and stitch textures to achieve a balance of form and harmony. This did not mean rejection of a new approach, a new development, or influence. The secure interpreter of stitch application alway understood that a new style was neither threat-

113

ening nor necessarily displeasing. Instead embroiderers throughout the ages, comfortable with color, familiar with a varied number of natural embroidery elements (spun and dyed by professionals or amateurs depending upon economic necessity), and sure of that technique, considered their embroidery a reflection of self. Absorbing the novel and the unusual into the familiar was spontaneous. Everyone knew that the investment of time for fine handwork was great. Only by the payment of minimal hourly wages or piecework rates to the perpetually available workforce of poor women and children did workshop owners and their journeymen have a cheap source of labor available. This was essential to their professional survival since there is much repetitive stitching within any piece of needlework. The time consuming process of producing both the essential and the decorative for a family or home was only possible within a society which limited the activities of its women to the home. Needlework as a "ladylike" occupation was a socio-economic development rather than an evolution of the craft. Women not pressed into the hard physical labor of providing for others in a rural economy had the time to embroider and the financial means to obtain the best in design and materials.

Today time is still a definite and essential component of all good needlework. Although embroidery by number (the kit), carefully market researched as to the quantity of mate-

rial and time required to complete it is promoted as the instant solution to expertise and a shortcut to skill, there is an increasing counterforce. The men and women who join local and national embroidery guilds and groups working for exhibitions—regardless of whether their personal taste leans to traditional or contemporary designs—seek a greater ease in self expression by stitching. Surely this is an indication that despite an increasingly mechanized and regimented environment the human spirit and pride in craftsmanship inevitably reasserts itself, even in the latter part of the twentieth century.

This book has been written for those who are willing to give time but often are hesitant and doubtful as to whether their personal judgment in the selection of stitches and color can be trusted. By an explanation of how stitches evolve, grow, and develop as the result of a simple shift of hand movement, and how to think in terms of color, it is hoped that many will take courage and increase their own initiative. Once shading and the most basic stitches are familiar friends, the matter of adding texture and considering how to choose or plan a design are simple matters. It is essential for the survival of good needlework that the embroiderer lose all awe or apprehension of one of mankind's most ancient and most civilizing of skills.

GLOSSARY

Backface—The underside of a primary fabric, not seen by the embroiderer while attaching stitches. The backface is also known as the "wrong side" of the material.

Blocking—The finishing process for an embroidery. At its simplest, the process involves the following: the piece is first dampened and rolled into thick toweling to absorb all excess moisture and then stretched and nailed, in the same way an art canvas is nailed, onto a board covered with a thin sheet of plastic; it is then left to dry. Though personal blocking techniques vary, as long as all materials are of top quality, canvas paints are colorfast, blocking presents few problems. Steam-ironing a piece of needlework, especially canvas or crewel work, distorts stitches and flattens texture.

Bullion—*See* Purl.

Canvas—An even-weave, open-mesh linen, cotton, or silk fabric woven of heavily starched (sized) elements and obtainable in a variety of mesh sizes. Sizes are gauged according to the number of holes per inch. Quality varies and depends on the weight, ply, and twist of the element used.

Canvas work—Embroidery with wool, silk, or cotton that employs the counted-thread system to completely cover an open-holed, primary fabric known as canvas. This form of embroidery is also known in the United States as needlepoint and in other parts of the world as tapestry or Gobelin embroidery.

Canvas-work wool—The wool used in canvas embroidery. It is obtainable in three sizes: 1)Thick rope-like elements often called tapestry wool, that are the result of twisting several spun threads into one and cannot be split for other sizes; 2) A three-ply wool consisting of three strands (each a double twist of spun threads), which can easily be separated and adapted to any canvas; 3) A thin, soft, two-ply (crewel) wool that cannot be split and is multiplied for use on large-size canvas mesh.

Wool should be judged by the natural sheen of its coloring, its resiliency, and its feel. Only long wool staples can be used for fine plied wools of soft texture. Short staples are spun and plied into thicker, hairier, and less flexible elements.

Continuous element—A piece of element of in-

115

determinate length, generally wound into a ball or onto a cone or weaving shuttle for knitting, weaving, crochet or tambour work.

Crossed loops—Any loop formed by moving the element behind the crossing of a loop of the previous row. Crossed loops are linked to the previous row.

Couching—The technique of tying down or fastening the laid element onto the fabric either in a pattern sequence or haphazardly by a series of wrapping stitches.

Counted thread work—The use of even-weave warp and weft elements as counting devices to regulate the shape and size of a stitch. This technique is common to all embroidery based on geometric shapes, such as cross stitch and canvas work.

Diapering—The art of repeating a stitch or series of stitches to form a design without a visible beginning or end except that defined by the outlines of the shape.

Down points—All points that are the result of the needle piercing the fabric from the front-face to the back (indicated by even numbers).

Drawn thread work—Withdrawing certain warp and/or weft elements from the primary fabric before employing standard hand movements to group or link the remaining elements into a design.

Element—A general term used to describe yarns, threads, and cords that are interworked with another in textile techniques such as weaving, embroidery, lace-making, etc.

Even weave (also plain or tabby weave)—A primary fabric with a balanced weave in which the warp and weft are evenly spaced, and identical in size and flexibility. In addition, the weft element has passed alternately over and under each successive warp element as it travels horizontally from one side of the warp to the other.

Fibers—Short lengths of hair, plant, or mineral matter that when spun together form yarns, threads, and cords.

Filament—A single, long thread or element derived from natural or manmade substances.

Floats—Long, loose stitches.

Frontface—The top side of a fabric which faces the needleworker while she attaches stitches. The frontface is also known as the "right side" of the material.

Guest element—In needlepoint, an element using the hole that belongs to another element.

Holes (or points)—The openings made by a needle as it pierces the primary fabric.

Host element—The element that belongs to previously formed stitch.

Inactive element—That section of an element between the two opposing extremes (working and passive) that rests on the primary fabric until drawn or pulled into position by the needle and the threaded end of the element.

Interconnected loops—Loops not only linked to one another row by row, but also side by side in the same row.

Interlooping—Drawing one loop through another.

Laid threads—Unworked lines of the embroidery element that are attached to the surface of the primary fabric.

Left-over-right-loop—A loop in which the left arm or leg of a loop lies over and therefore crosses the lower right arm.

Linen twill—A weave of organized floats or skips with continuous diagonals. This sturdy background material is manufactured in Ireland, Scotland, and Belgium. Quality can be judged by its weight as a piece is handled, and by the sheen of its finish.

Link—That segment of any element joining one part to another.

Linking—A primary frontface technique in which an already completed stitch is connected to the starting point of the next by sliding the needle behind that segment of the element resting on the surface of the primary fabric.

Loop—A circular shape resulting from layering one end of an embroidery element across another.

Monocanvas (also unicanvas)—Single mesh as opposed to penelope canvas.

Needlepoint—The hole one makes into a fabric with a threaded needle or a lace made with needle and thread. For centuries the word *needlepoint* has defined a lace worked with needle and thread instead of bobbins, and its common use to define canvas work in the United States is a curious redefinition of its true meaning.

Passing—Embroidery elements produced by winding thin strips of gold, silver, or other substance around a core of silk.

Passive element—The other end of the working element, which is either attached to the primary fabric or interworked in another stitch and thereby restricted in its ability to follow the needle's movement.

Penelope canvas—Double-mesh canvas obtainable in equal and unequal warp/weft spacing. The former is primarily intended for counted thread work, while the latter assures elongated, slanted, or diagonal stitches. Two measurements or gauges are used to evaluate its size, the number of large holes per inch and the number of smaller holes per inch obtained by prying all double elements apart with a blunt needle.

Plain weave—*See* Even weave.

Plied yarns or threads—The element resulting from twisting together a specific number of single yarns.

Points—*See* Holes.

Primary fabric—Any material, regardless of structure, quality, or texture, into which a stitch can be worked, or onto which a stitch can be attached with a needle and a suitable element.

Pull—The hand movement required to draw the entire length of an embroidery element through the primary fabric, a loop, or another stitch.

Purl (also bullion)—Gold or silver wire twisted into a continuous spiral rope. Obtainable in a variety of thicknesses and finishes, pieces of a required size are cut off, threaded like beads, and sewn onto a fabric.

Quality of ply—The firmness of a set of plied or re-plied elements which is measured by the number of twists per inch and the resulting slant or angle of each twist.

Right-over-left-loop—A loop in which the right arm or leg of the loop lies over and moves across the left arm.

Seeding—Scattering a single stitch or a set of stitches in a haphazard manner to darken or lighten certain areas within a motif or to break up the intensity of the color of the primary fabric without the formality of a design.

Shadow breaks—The breaks between stitches at the point of entry of the element into the fabric that, if taken into consideration, can provide the three-dimensional sculptural impact unique to certain textile techniques.

Single yarn—The long, drawn out, and spun thread.

Sizing—The starch required to stiffen canvas so that the holes remain open; it dissolves when the finished piece is blocked into shape. The use of a sizing of rice starch or glue to smooth a finished and blocked textile is not recommended by the conservation department of the Textile Museum.

Spangles—Sequins are the present-day equivalent of spangles.

Spun elements—Elements formed from short lengths of fiber laid parallel and then pulled and twisted together into a continuous thread.

Stepping sequence—A needlework technique in which each new stitch row or stitch is moved above or below a preceding line and to the left or to the right of its predecessor.

Stitch—A shape, textile fiber structure, or accessory attached to a primary fabric as the result of moving an embroidery element in, out, and around a segment of its interlaced structure.

Stitch line—The direction taken by a series of contiguous stitches.

Stitch row—A complete line of stitches.

Stitch unit—Any complete shape or stitch form irrespective of whether it requires one basic up and down hand movement, several identical or similar repeats, or the addition of other motions before it achieves its correct form.

S-twist—Plied elements spiraling together from upper left to lower right.

Tabby weave—*See* Even weave.

Tension—The art and skill of maintaining an even rhythm in the pull and tug of the working element as the needle is manipulated in and out of the primary fabric so that all resulting stitches are identical in size, width, height, texture, and spacing. Any deviation from such a norm must be intentional rather than due to lack of manual skill.

Three-part stitch construction—Stitches owing their development to the combined use of a definite sequence of basic needlework hand movements derived from simple stitch techniques. Sometimes a stitch construction has more than three parts.

Tug—The action of giving a sharp pull to a short length of the passive end of the embroidery element to withdraw any excess slack and thereby retain an even tension.

Turning a work—Depending upon the recommended technique of the stitch line, this instruction requires the embroidery fabric to be turned in the hand either 90 or 180 degrees before a new row of stitching is started.

Twisted filament—Two or more filaments twisted together to form a single unit.

Two-part stitch construction—A stitch shape resulting from the use of two dissimilar hand movements.

Unbalanced weave—The opposite of a plain weave.

Unicanvas—Fine-weave monocanvas.

Up points—All points that are the result of the needle pushing from the backface to the front (indicated by uneven numbers unless otherwise stated).

Warp—A set of long, parallel elements stretched from one end of the weaving loom to the other to support a second set of elements known as the "weft."

Weft—Elements that are interworked with and cross the warp horizontally, thereby creating a fabric.

Weaving—The interlacing of warp and weft.

Working element—The free end of a piece of yarn or thread, which, after being threaded on a needle, follows the needle's movements as it is pushed in and out of the primary fabric to develop a stitch.

Z-twist—Plied elements spiraling from lower left to upper right.

BIBLIOGRAPHY

Alford, Lady M. *Needlework as Art.*

Anchor Manual of Needlework. London: B. T. Batsford, 1958, 1970.

A. R. *Designs for Church Embroidery.* London: Chapman & Hall, 1894.

Art Needlework. A Complete Manual of Embroidery in Silks and Crewels. London: Ward Lock & Co., 1891.

Ashley, Clifford W. *The Ashley Book of Knots.* London: Faber and Faber, 1944.

Barber, Giles. *Textile and Embroidered Bookbindings.* Oxford: Bodleian Library, 1971.

Battaglia, Heidi Haupt, and Haupt, Paul. *Komm Wir Sticken.* Bern: Haupt.

———. *Wir Sticken Weiter.* Bern: Haupt.

Bordados Populares Espanoles. Madrid: Maravillas Segura Lacourba, 1949.

Carita. *Lacis—Filet Brode or Darning on a Net.* London: Sampson, Low, Marston & Co., 1909.

Caulfield, S. F. A., and Saward, B. C. *Dictionary of Needlework.* London: L. Upcott Gill, 1882.

Cave, Oenone. *English Folk Embroidery.* London: Mills & Boon, Ltd., 1965.

Charles, M., and Pages, L. *Les Broderies et les Dentelles.* Paris: Librairie Felix Juven, 1905.

Christie, Mrs. A. H. *Embroidery and Tapestry Weaving.* 4th ed. London: John Hogg, 1915.

Colby, Averil. *Samplers.* London: B. T. Batsford, Ltd. 1964.

Cole, Alan S. *Descriptive Catalogue of Collections of Tapestry & Embroidery in the South Kensington Museum.* London: Her Majesty's Stationary Office, 1888.

Cox, Hebe. *Canvas Embroidery.* London: Mills & Boon, Ltd., 1960.

Czarnecka, Irene. *Folk Art in Poland.* Warsaw; 1957.

Day, Lewis F., and Buckle, Mary. *Art in Needlework.* 2nd rev. ed. London: B. T. Batsford, 1901.

Day, Lewis F. *Everyday Art*. London: B. T. Batsford, 1882.

Dean, Beryl. *Ecclesiastical Embroidery*. London: B. T. Batsford, 1958.

Digby, George Wingfield. *Elizabethan Embroidery*. London: Faber & Faber, 1963.

de Dillmont, Therese. *Encyclopedie des Ouvrages de Dames*. 1st ed. Mulhouse (Alsace): Brustlein & Cie.

————. *Encyklopaedie der Weiblichen Handarbeiten*. new rev. ed. Mulhouse (Alsace): Therese de Dillmont Bibliothek DMC, 1912.

de Zuluetta, Francis. *Embroideries by Mary Stuart and Elizabeth Talbot at Oxburgh Hall*. Oxford: Oxford University Press, 1923.

Ditchfield, P. H. *The City Companies of London and their Good Works*. London: J. M. Dent & Co., 1904.

Dolby, Anastasia. *Church Embroideries*. London: Chapman & Hall, 1867.

Dongerkery, Kamala S. *The Romance of Indian Embroidery*. Bombay: Thacker & Co., 1951.

Eivor Fisher Coats Sewing Group. *Swedish Embroidery*. London: B. T. Batsford, 1962.

Elizabethan Embroidery. London: Victoria & Albert Museum.

Embroidery, vol. 1. London: James Pearsall & Co., 1923-33.

Emery, Irene. *The Primary Structures of Fabric: An Illustrated Classification*. Washington, D. C.: The Textile Museum, 1967.

Enthoven, Jacqueline. *Stitchery for Children*. New York: Van Nostrand Reinhold Co., 1968.

————. *The Stitches of Creative Embroidery*. New York: Van Nostrand Reinhold Co., 1964.

Fangel, Esther. *Pulled Threadwork*. Copenhagen: Host & Sons Forlag, 1958.

Fitzwilliam, Ada Wentworth, and Hands, A. F. Morris. *Jacobean Embroidery*. London: Kegan, Paul, French Trubner & Co., Ltd., 1912.

Foris, Maria & Andreas (The pattern collection of), with text by H. E. Kiewe, *History of Folk Cross Stitch*. Nuremberg: Sebaldus Verlag, 1950.

The Franco-British Exhibition of Textiles. London: Victoria & Albert Museum, 1921.

Geddes, Elisabeth. *Design for Flower Embroidery*. London: Mills & Boon, Ltd., 1961.

Geddes & McNeill. *Black Work*. London: Mills & Boon, Ltd., 1961.

Gibbon, M. A. *Canvas Work*. A. Bell.

Gulgowski, Seefried. *Landlicher Hausfleiss*. Berlin: Deutsche Landbuchhandlung GMBH, 1914.

Hackenbrock, Yvonne. *English and other needlework, tapestries and textiles in the Irwin Untermeyer Collection*. London: Thames and Hudson, 1960.

Hands, H. M. *Church Needlework*. London: The Faith Press, Ltd., 1909.

Hansen, H. J. *European Folk Art*. London: Thames & Hudson, 1968.

Higgin, L. *Handbook of Embroidery*. London: Sampson, Low, Marston, Searle & Rivington, 1880.

Hiler, Hilaire. *Introduction to the Study of Costume from Nudity to Raiment*. London: W. & G. Foyle, Ltd., 1929.

Howard, Constance. *Design for Embroidery from Traditional English Sources*. London: B. T. Batsford, 1956.

Hughes, Jessie. *Embroidery*. London: Evans Practical Handbook, 1963.

Johnstone, Pauline. *Greek Island*. London: Alec Trianti, 1961.

————. *Byzantine Tradition in Church Embroidery*. London: Alec Trianti, 1967.

Karasz, Mariska. *Adventures in Stitches*. New York: Funk & Wagnalls.

Kendrick, A. F. *English Needlework*. London: A. & C. Black, 1933.

————. *English Decorative Fabrics of the 16th and 18th Centuries.* London: F. Lewis, Ltd., 1934.

Kiewe, Heinz E., with Biddulph, Michael, and Woods, Victor. *Civilization on Loan.* Oxford: A. N. I. Art Needlework Industries, Ltd., 1973.

Klickman, Flora. *The Home Art Book of Fancy Stitchery.* London: Girls' Own Paper, 1920s.

L . . ., Charlotte. *Handbuchlein zur angenehmen und nützlichen Beschäftigung für junge Damen.* Ilmenau: Voigt, 1831.

Levey, Santina. *Embroidery of the 19th Century.* Tring, Herts: Shire Publications, 1971.

Liley, Alison. *The Craft of Embroidery.* London: Mills & Boon, Ltd., 1961.

————. *Embroidery—A Fresh Approach.* London: Mills & Boon, Ltd., 1964.

Lockwood, M. S., and Glaister, E. *Art Embroidery.* London: Marcus Ward & Co., 1878.

Loves, Mary Eirwen. *The Romance of Lace.* Staples Publication.

Mackie, Louise W. *The Splendour of Turkish Weaving.* Washington, D.C.: The Textile Museum, 1973.

Mann, Kathleen. *Peasant Costume in Europe.* London: A & C Black, Ltd., 1935.

Masters, Ellen T. *The Book of Stitches.* London: James Bowden, 1899.

Needle and Thread, periodical. London: James Pearsall & Co. No. I, March, 1914; No. III, July, 1914.

Norbury, James. *Counted Thread Embroidery.* Leicester: Brockhampton Press, 1955.

Norwick, B. "The Origins of Knitting." *Knitting Times.* Vol. 40, May, 1971.

Nuova Enciclopedia del Lavori Famminili. 3rd ed. Milan: Edition Mani di Fata.

Old English Needlework of the 16th and 17th Century. London: Sidney Hand, Ltd.

Owen and Wilson. *Illuminated Book of Needlework.* Covent Garden: Henry Bohen, 1877.

Pass, Olivia. *Dorset Feather Stitchery.* London: Mills & Boon, Ltd., 1957.

Pesel, L. *Portfolio of Stitches,* vol. 1: Old English; vol. 2: Eastern; vol. 3: Western. Bradford: Percy, Lund, Humphries and Coe, Ltd., 1921.

Petersen, Grete, and Svennas, Elsie. *Handbook of Stitches.* New York: Van Nostrand Reinhold, & Co., 1966.

Roseveas, Elizabeth. *Needlework, Knitting, Cutting Out.* London: MacMillan & Co., 1894.

Schimmelmann. *Volkstumliche Handwebtechniken.* Stuttgart: Kanradies Verlag, 1954.

Schuette, Marie and Muller-Christensen, Sigrid. *The Art of Embroidery.* London: Thames & Hudson, 1964.

Schwetter, Bertha. *Beyer Handarbeitsbuch.* Wiesbaden: Beyer Verlag, 1963.

Snook, Barbara. *The Creative Art of Embroidery.* London: B. T. Batsford, Ltd.

————. *Embroidery Stitches.* London: B. T. Batsford, Ltd.,1960.

————. *Learning to Embroider.* London: B. T. Batsford, Ltd.

Stiaony, Emilie. *Stickerel—Techniken fur Schuler Praxis.* Vienna: K. K. Lehrmittel-bureau für Gewerbliche Unterrichtanstalten, 1910.

Stearns, Martha Genung. *Homespun & Blue.* New York: Charles Scribners, 1940.

Symonds, Mary. *Elementary Embroidery.* London: John Hogg, 1915.

Symonds, Mary, and Preece, Louise. *Needlework through the Ages.* London: Hoddes & Stoughton, 1928.

Thesiger, Ernest. *Adventures in Embroidery.* London: London Studio, 1941.

Thomas, Mary. *Dictionary of Embroidery Stitches.* Gramercy Publishing Co.

————. Embroidery Book. Gramercy Publishing Co., 1934.

Trianti, Alec, and Tebbs, L. R. *The New Punto Tagliato Embroidery Supplement.* London: Chapman & Hall, Ltd., 1913.

Townsend, W. G. Paulson. *Embroidery, or The Craft of the Needle.* London: Truslove,

Hanson & Comba, Ltd., 1899.

Ullemayer, Rudolph, and Tidow, Klaus. *Die Textil und Lederfunde Der Grabung Feddersen Wierde.*

"Probleme der Kustenforschung im sudlichen Nordseegebiet." Sonderdruck. Vol. 10 Hildesheim: Verlagsbuchhandlung August Lax, 1973.

Urquhart, H., and Hindson, A. *Seal-Bags in Treasury Canterbury Cathedral, 1934.* London: London Antiquaries, 1935.

Voshage, Adele. *Das Spitzen Kloppeln.* Hanover, 1894.

Waring, Mary E. *An Embroidery Pattern Book.* London: Pittman, 1931.

Wilton, Countess of. *Art of Needlework.* London: Henry Colburn, 1840.

Wheeler, Candace. *Development of Embroidery in America.* New York: Harper's , 1921.

Whyte, Kathleen. *Design in Embroidery.* New York: B. T. Batsford, Ltd., 1969.

The Young Ladies' Journal Guide to the Worktable. London: James Pearsall & Co., 1886.